Stress, Coping, and Health

KU-624-962

This Book was
Donated to the
Learning Centre by
NE Lincs Council

LOCATION

ACC.
No.

Grimsby Institute

121064

Meinrad Perrez, PhD

After studies in Paris, Innsbruck, and Salzburg, Meinrad Perrez became a research assistant at the University of Salzburg in 1971. Shortly afterwards he was called to the Free University of Berlin as a full professor. In 1976 he became professor at the University of Fribourg, Switzerland, where he was appointed head of the department of clinical psychology in 1981. He is regularly invited to lecture at major universities throughout Europe. From 1987 to 1989 he was president of the Swiss Society for Psychology, and he is currently on the editorial board of several journals in the field of psychology. His contributions to stress research focus especially on the assessment of stress behavior in natural settings.

Michael Reicherts, PhD

After his master in economics in 1975, Michael Reicherts became a research assistant at the University of Cologne. He continued his academic career by studying psychology at the University of Bonn, where he became a research assistant in this field in 1982. His PhD studies then brought him to the University of Fribourg, Switzerland. He presently works as a scientific collaborator with professor Perrez. Among many other works, he is the author of a monograph on Psychological Assessment of Stress and Coping Behavior.

Richard S. Lazarus, PhD

Richard S. Lazarus received his PhD in experimental psychology from the University of Pittsburgh in 1948. He was an assistant professor at Johns Hopkins University from 1948 to 1953, an associate professor at Clark University from 1953 to 1957, and has been a full professor at the University of California at Berkeley since 1959. His chief interests are in the fields of process-oriented stress research. He was a key pioneer in the area of modern cognitive stress research, and is today one of the most important leaders in this field.

LOCATION	HE
CLASS No.	155·9042
ACC. No.	121064

WITHDRAWN

Cover design by Andrea Schedle.

Stress, Coping, and Health

A Situation-Behavior Approach
Theory, Methods, Applications

by

Meinrad Perez & Michael Reicherts
University of Fribourg, Switzerland

Foreword by

Richard S. Lazarus

 Hogrefe & Huber Publishers
Seattle • Toronto • Bern • Göttingen

Library of Congress Cataloging-in-Publication Data

Perrez, Meinrad.
    Stress, coping, and health : a situation-behavior approach :
theory, methods, applications / by Meinrad Perrez and Michael
Reicherts ; foreword by Richard S. Lazarus.
        p.   cm.
    Includes bibliographical references and index.
    ISBN 0-88937-065-6 : $39.00
    !. Stress (Psychology) 2. Adjustment (Psychology) 3. Personality
and situation. 4. Clinical health psychology. I. Reicherts,
Michael, 1950-   . II. Title.
    [DNLM: 1. Adaptation, Psychological. 2. Psychological Theory.
3. Stress, Psychological--prevention & control.   WM 172 P455s]
BF575.S75P45 1992
155.9'042--dc20
DNLM/DLC
for Library of Congress   92-35352
                                                                    CIP

Canadian Cataloguing in Publication Data

    Perrez, Meinrad
        Stress, coping and health

    Includes bibliographical references and index.
    ISBN 0-88937-065-6

    1. Stress (Psychology). 2. Adjustment (Psychology).
    I. Reicherts, Michael, 1950-   . II. Title.

    BF575.S75P47 .1992   155.9'042   C92-095563-8

No part of this book may be reproduced, stored in a retrieval system, or transmitted,
in any form or by any means, electronic, mechanical, photocopying, microfilming,
recording or otherwise, without the written permission from the publisher.

© Copyright 1992 by Hogrefe & Huber Publishers

Seattle Office   12 Bruce Park Avenue
P.O. Box 2487   Toronto, Ontario
Kirkland, WA 98083-2487   M4P 2S3
(206) 820-1500

ISBN 0-88937-065-6
ISBN 3-456-82081-X
Hogrefe & Huber Publishers
Seattle • Toronto • Bern • Göttingen

Printed in the United States of America

Table of contents

Preface and overview

The following text is the provisional result of the joint research carried out by the two authors over the last five years. Two ideas were paramount in our approach. The first concerns the impact of situation. The role of situational features - both objective and subjective - has to be studied, to achieve a better understanding of adaptational processes. How can we define a particular response as adaptive in the absence of any knowledge about the nature of the stressor to which the subject was reacting? What are the psychologically relevant factors of stressful situations? We assume that it is possible to describe functional relationships between some characteristics of stressors and suitable adaptive responses which can be subject of empirical research. How is it possible to get a rationally founded idea about people's coping competences without taking into consideration different types of coping tasks for which they may be more or less able? Someone may be very competent at mastering controllable stressors - Type-A people for example - but the same person may be quite incompetent in dealing with uncontrollable situations. Secondly, we were interested in developing a new methodology for looking at stress and coping. How can we reconstruct process aspects of coping behavior with psychological instruments? How can we obtain more reliable information about coping with stress in everyday situations?

It can clearly be seen that essential aspects of our theoretical framework are based on the work of Richard S. Lazarus, in particular his conceptualization of stress and coping behaviors as *processes* related to the *appraisal* of the situation. For his valuable foreword to the book we thank him very much.

Some of the chapters are based on publications in European journals and books and are integrated in the text in a reworked form.

We would like to thank many people and institutions for their help and support: Robert Matathia and Bernard Plancherel for numerous discussions and for support in programming and elaboration of data. We think back with delight to the stimulating discussions with

Richard S. Lazarus on the shore of lake Geneva. We will not forget the productive exchanges with Heinz W. Krohne and with Klaus R. Scherer. Shirley Fisher, John B. Davies and members of the Center of Occupational and Health Psychology of the University of Strathclyde and Rudolf H. Schaffer, the head of Strathclyde's Department of Psychology, will be especially remembered for their generous help and the excellent intellectual and human environment they provided over several months in the summer of 1990, in Glasgow. David Shewan and his colleagues at the Center helped to bridge the linguistic ditch improving our first versions of the text. Paul Gilbert from the Pastures Hospital, Mickleover/Derby, proposed final corrections. We are indebted to our British friends for their tireless help and to Emma Moreno Puy for her second case study example which she was experiencing under the eyes of one of the authors.

Special thanks should also be extended to the Swiss National Foundation for the Advancement of Scientific Research, to the Council of the University of Fribourg and to the British Academy for their financial support. Last but not least, we should not forget that Peter Stehlin of Hogrefe & Huber Publishers assisted in a very helpful way to realize the publication of the manuscript.

Overview

The book consists of three main parts: Theoretical framework, New approaches to the assessment, and Applications in clinical and health psychology. There are also the fictive *case studies of Harry and Evelyn* interwoven with the main parts to illustrate the theoretical approach, the assessment methods, and the applications to health psychology.

Part I, *Theoretical framework*, takes into account that the analysis of stress and coping has to refer to situational features. Stressors are considered as coping tasks with specific situational demands - if stress reduction is intended. The framework focuses on concrete stressful episodes as the units of analysis.

Part II, *New approaches to the assessment*, begins with the description of a *process questionnaire* (chapter 2). The aim of this instrument is to present the subject with prototypical stressful situation-sequences (S-R-

S-R tasks) standardized and described by objective parameters. It deals with the subject's perception of these situations and the related emotional, cognitive and behavioral responses. In chapter 3, an empirical study is presented which analyses the impact of situational and process factors (and their interaction) on the response patterns of stress and coping as modeled by this instrument.

In chapter 4 we describe the construction of a *computer-aided self-observation method*. This second instrument operates within the same theoretical structure as the questionnaire. It works not through preformed hypothetical situations, but with actual everyday situations experienced by the participant. The subject has to record the way he or she perceives stressful situations, as well as his/her emotional, cognitive and behavioral response pattern. Initial results concerning the reliability, reactivity and validity of this method are reported. In chapter 5, the method is applied to test its ability to predict stress and coping behavior in the natural setting.

While chapters 2 and 4 concern an introduction to methodological issues and the construction of the new instruments, chapter 3 and 5, give initial evidence about their validation within the framework of the situation-behavior theory (theoretical assumptions) of part I.

In part III, *Applications*, the basic theoretical ideas are applied to different areas of clinical and health psychology. Chapters 6, 7, and 8 are based on questionnaire data. They deal with coping behavior in depression, i.e. the ways of coping with aversive events (chapter 6) and with loss and failure (chapter 7) and compare depressed and non-depressed people.

Chapter 8 describes coping tendencies as a buffering factor in the stress experience of people infected with HIV. Chapters 9 and 10 concern the coping tendencies of students related to different criteria of mental health, and stress as experienced of the members of an institution, of a medical unit. Both use the computer-assisted self-observation method.

Finally, a new concept to analyse adequate coping behavior - emerging from the previous considerations and results - is outlined (chapter 11). It aims at the foundation of behavior rules which recommend coping behavior appropriate to the stressful situation.

The different parts in the book can be read independently: The reader may start with theory and methods. But he or she could also begin with part III, dealing with the theory in practice. Alternatively, the case studies may be useful in providing a step-by-step introduction to the main text.

Meinrad Perrez and Michael Reicherts,
University of Fribourg/Switzerland

Foreword

Richard S. Lazarus

Research and theory on the coping process are still in their infancy. A new approach to coping, which is transactional, contextual and process-centered, began to appear in the late 1970's, stimulated by cognitive-relational theories of stress and emotion, which were a part of the broad cognitive movement in psychology, and which began to take shape in the 1960's with the pioneering work of Janis (1958), Arnold (1960), Mechanic (1962) and myself (Lazarus, 1966). Although tracing history is always a risky business, I believe that this movement was an extension of the important theoretical and metatheoretical work of at least two prior generations of writers who emphasized phenomenological, field theoretical, systems theory, personalistic, and social learning concepts, including Harlow (1953), Heider (1958), Kelly (1955), Lewin (1935), McClelland (1951), Murphy (1947), Murray (1938), Rotter (1966), and White (1959).

Earlier thinking about coping, and coping measurement, featured a psychoanalytical ego-psychology outlook in which the emphasis was placed on coping as a personality style, usually in the form of broad dichotomies of defensive strategies such as repression-sensitization. One or another of these styles were assumed to characterize the person. One problem with this is that most people fall in the middle of the style dimension, being neither extreme repressors or sensitizers, so that finding a strong style was also tantamount to finding a highly rigid and pathological coping pattern.

Such styles of coping were also regarded hierarchically as ranging from healthy (termed coping) to progressively more unhealthy or dysfunctional (called defenses), for example, neurotic or psychotic. Thus, certain forms of coping (e.g. denial) were automatically considered to be pathological and pathogenic and others healthy or nearly so. And because it was postulated in advance which forms of coping were healthy or pathological, the coping process was not assessed independently of the adaptational outcome with the resulting problem that it was not possible to evaluate the functional or dysfunctional outcomes of the process and thus to determine the conditions under which coping or defense (e.g., denial) might have positive as well as negative adaptational value for the individual.

The most serious deficiency of this earlier coping theory was that it was not possible to study and describe in detail how the person coped in thought and action with specific stresses such as illness, personal loss, and inter- and intra-psychic threats which might occur in specific contexts of living. Clinical workers need to know how a client is dealing with this or that specific stress, which might vary with the nature of the stress or its environmental context, in addition to considering the stable overall style within which the relationship with the world is conceived and managed.

That is, even if we know that an individual is generally effective in coping and as a personality that individual has the advantage of positive coping resources such as intelligence, skill, supportive family and social relationships, money, and health, this will not help us greatly to teach those who cope poorly to do better unless we also know what it is specifically that both kinds of persons do and think when coping. We need to know precisely what it is that works and does not work in particular kinds of persons, in particular kinds of stress, and in particular environmental contexts of living in order to discover what to teach about coping. This means that modern coping theory and research must become more detailed and descriptive than it has been in the past.

What is distinctive about the more recent work on coping is that it seeks to describe the coping thought and acts which occur in specific stressful encounters on the premise, now well-documented, that the coping process can change with the demands of each new encounter, and over time, as the person-environment relationship changes. This means that although there are personality-based stabilites in the ways individual persons cope across occasions and time, as Perrez and Reicherts document in their research, stability is bound to be somewhat limited because of the changing requirements of coping, as these are perceived and appraised by persons.

Since I have now curtailed my empirical work on stress and coping (which was summarized in Lazarus and Folkman, 1984; 1987), it is very gratifying to find that it has stimulated a number of major efforts, such as those of Perrez and Reicherts, to carry stress and coping theory and research beyond the point where Folkman and I were able to take it. Although there are many important issues yet to be resolved about how best to measure appraisal and coping and their adaptational outcomes, and much ongoing research is being reported, relatively little of it is programmatic or committed to modifying or expanding the theory. It is, therefore, a pleasure to have the opportunity to write a foreword to this book because the research and ideas reported are, in my opinion, serious and successful efforts to advance our understanding of the stress and coping process beyond previous work.

Perrez and Reicherts' book begins with a chapter on theory, proceeds with some chapters on method, then offers a series of empirical studies that draw on the theory and method, followed by integrating discussions about the prediction of coping in the natural setting and about what constitutes effective coping.

In examining what Perrez and Reicherts have done, three themes are of particular importance.

I. They seek to distinguish - in theory - the *objective parameters* of situations, which are important in adaptation, from *subjective perceptions*, which includes what I mean by appraisal. This is a noteworthy aim because the fit or misfit of appraisal and coping with the requirements presented by the environment is important for good and poor functioning. How to distinguish between the objective and the subjective is a perrenial and very deep issue in social science, and it remains difficult to resolve. The authors confront this directly and with vitality.

What Perrez and Reicherts say, soundly I believe, is that for good adaptation there must also a good fit between the objective situation and the subjective perceptions and appraisals (see also Lazarus & Folkman, 1984). This presupposes a more or less adequate perception of the important features of the environment, as well as the choice of appropriate coping strategies for dealing with them. The authors conceptualize and draw a number of important situational features of stressful encounters such as controllability, changeability, and ambiguity. In their questionnaire to study appraisal and coping they employ effectively hypothetical situations and emphasize subjective perceptions of those parameters.

II. The authors also make an important contribution to coping theory by adding to the as yet too simple taxonomy used by Lazarus and Folkman. The major addition was inspired by Perrez and Reicherts' concern with the relevant properties of situations, which they divide into internal or external demands which disturb homeostasis. Coping behavior is then classified in accordance with whether it is centered on the *situation*, the subjective representation of the situation, or the volitional (or motivational) dimension of the stressful encounter. If the coping is centered on the situation, it may be either instrumental, passive, or evasive; if it centers on the *cognitive representation*, it may take the form of either information-seeking or information suppressing; if it centers on *volition*, the alternative coping possibilities are either re-evaluation or changing of the goal.

These additions provide a potentially important expansion of the two functions of coping I have emphasized, problem-focused and emotion-focused, and the eight coping strategies that emerged from factor analyses of the Ways of Coping scale (Folkman & Lazarus, 1988). These additional concepts and dimensions point out that our present understanding of the coping process may be incomplete and provides opportunities for continuing modifications and advances at the conceptual level.

III. In addition to new theoretical contributions, there is also room for advances in method, and Perrez and Reicherts offer an extremely important one in this book. One of the difficulties in the measurement of coping has been that the best and most naturalistic strategies of measurement depend on retrospective analysis of stressful encounters that have taken place a day, a week, or month ago, which leaves much room for the distortions produced by forgetting and retrospective falsification. The authors created a computer-aided procedure in which experiential field data are stored in a pocket computer which subjects carry with them in their daily round of adaptations. This procedure is a very useful variant of the 'beeper' methodology in which, at a signal, subjects are asked to answer questions for data collection. In this case, the portable computer makes it possible to obtain and store psychological information with minimal time delay between the events of interest and the research inquiry about their stressful implications and the coping process involved.

This computer-aided self observation makes use of a series of standardized questions about the stressful transaction, based on variables of interest such as appraised controllability and coping choices. The program, written for a pocket computer with a four-line display, presents the subject with these interview questions, which are answered as soon as possible after the transaction. This makes it possible to conduct the interview-based assessment in the field setting in which stressful encounters occur, to obtain the responses to them shortly after the encounter, and to store the data for computation later. In this way, a persons' appraisals and coping reactions can be related with more certainty to the properties of the stressful encounters being studied.

I believe what has been reported in this book constitutes an important contribution to stress and coping theory and research and I expect that it will have a major influence on this important field of inquiry.

Richard S. Lazarus,
University of California, Berkeley/USA

Case studies

Introduction

In everyday life we can be confronted with various types of stressful and undesirable events. These can include: having to go for job interviews, getting loss in a strange city, having a car accident, taking examinations, becoming unemployed, loss of a loving relationship, being threatened by a stranger, having ones home broken into - and so forth. These situations and events automatically elicit some kind of response, 'what should we do'? The way we think about the event or situation, that is what it means to us, and the response we choose to deal with it can vary enormously. This variation can arise from the situation itself and/or the personal subjective meaning of the situation. Thus, as seems self-evident, we are unlikely to deal with being lost in a strange city in the same way as losing someone close to us. In other words, situations have their own characteristics. Also people will vary in their response to the same situation. For one person being lost in a strange city is a minor irritation but for another it elicits panic. Someone about to inherit a million pounds may be less anxious about exams than a poor person whose whole life has revolved around a good career. Consequently, factors relevant to both situations themselves and personal appraisal will contribute to a person's adaptation and state of health.

As noted in the preface, this book attempts to explore various ways that these differences, in both situation and person factors, can be distinguished, operationalised and studied scientifically. We aim to outline a classification system that pays due regard to both situation variability and person variability - that is coping. Further we shall outline a new methodology that enables us to work closely at the points in time when stress occurs. We will also explore various health issues. But first, to highlight the potential for these twin sources of variation, let us explore two examples of a stressful event.

Two stressful examples

Harry is lost

Imagine a young man - named Harry - visiting a foreign city for the first time. He has an important appointment at 10 a.m. with the director of a firm. He has been invited for interview. He really wants to get this post - it's important to him. He starts out from the hotel at a quarter past nine, convinced that he can reach his destination on foot in 30 minutes. However, after having walked through the streets for more than 20 minutes he realizes he is going the wrong way. He now asks a woman to tell him the way to the little street where the firm has its head office, but she is unable to help him. The next person, a road worker, has no idea about the whereabouts of this little street either. The young man begins to get upset about his situation. If he lost his main chance to get the post because of being late, he would really regret it - and his wife would never forget it too. No taxi is available. He realizes that he will never make it on foot, irrespective of being lost. Then he thinks 'Let's try to find somebody who can drive me there... I still have a chance!' He decides to ask a man just getting into his car, if he can help him in his complicated situation. Harry didn't succeed with his first attempt. The third car driver he asks knows the street and takes him there.

This young man experienced a stressful situation which began when he realised he was lost and was in danger of being late for an important appointment. His reaction was both emotional and intellectual, and led to his finding a solution to his predicament.

Evelyn lost her earring

Evelyn is playing golf with her friends. She is wearing a pair of precious earrings. A short time after having finished her game she suddenly becomes aware that she has lost one of her earrings. She feels worried and annoyed with herself for having lost it and runs back to the golf-course to search for the lost present she had worn today for only the second time. After having searched high and low for the missing earring she realizes she will never find that tiny precious present her mother had given her a few days before. Evelyn begins to feel sad and sighs. Then she takes a deep breath and tells herself:

'All I can do is inform the owner of the golf-course. The chances of seeing it again are remote. It is unfortunate, but it can't be helped and besides, there are more important things in life. I suppose I'll just have to tell my mother.'

Again, this woman was placed in a stressful situation of the sort we have all experienced. She was confronted with the loss of a loved and irrecoverable object. She reacts emotionally and tries to cope with the situation actively first, then by a kind of philosophical acceptance.

What can the psychology of stress contribute to a better understanding of such events? How can episodes like the above be conceptualized by a psychological framework? Can psychology enrich our understanding of everyday experiences like those described in our case examples?

The following chapters are designed to give some answers to such questions. Theoretical considerations, new methodological approaches, and empirical results will be examined in view of the fictional stressful episodes of Harry and Evelyn. We conclude the different parts of the book by re-assessing the case examples in line with the theoretical, methodological and empirical results presented.

PART I

THEORETICAL FRAMEWORK

1. A situation-behavior approach to stress and coping

Meinrad Perrez and Michael Reicherts

Introduction

Under the influence of the Berkeley group of R.S. Lazarus, the development of the psychological analysis of stress, coping and adaptation has been subject to fertile differentiations at the phenomenological level. Since the sixties, Lazarus (1966) has pointed out the significance of cognitive factors for coping with stress. He and his group have also emphasised the importance of the process involved in coping. In wide areas of psychological stress research, the distinctions between 'primary and secondary appraisal', 'problem- and emotion-focused coping' and 'appraisal and reappraisal' are part of today's basic vocabulary. The Berkeley group has succeeded in documenting the relevance of cognitive aspects for the interpretation of stressors and their influence on emotion (Lazarus, 1982, 1984; Lazarus & Smith, 1988). On the level of coping reactions, the distinction between system-related (internal) and system-external behavioral performances has proved useful for the study of adaptation processes.

The guiding rationale of Lazarus and his team was to set out a descriptive, phenomenological research program which drew attention to the individuality of these processes.

Referring to essential differentiations made by the Berkeley group, we are interested in the *lawful relations* between different psychological features in the coping process. For this, the newer control theories (Rotter, 1972; Seligman, 1975; Bandura, 1977; Fisher, 1984) seem to yield fruitful suggestions. We assume that a theory about coping with stress also has to include the significance of objective characteristics of the stressor. The following paragraphs are intended to provide a theoretical outline for the explanation and prediction of certain coping tendencies.

What are stressors or stressful situations?

When a stressful event occurs homeostasis is disturbed. The disturbance begins with the perception of a stressor. Stressors represent discontinuities in configurations of situation characteristics. These inner or outer changes condition the organism to respond through their intensity and/or duration. Characteristics of the stressor can be distinguished from the organism's perception of these characteristics. The stressors can be *internal* or *external* in origin. The disturbance of homeostasis can arise from characteristics of the stressor and the perception of it. The organism reacts to the perceived disturbance with automatic adaptive responses, or - depending on the type and extent of the disturbance - with adaptive actions that are goal-directed and potentially conscious. We call the whole situation-behavior sequence, or situation-action sequence, including its immediate - positive or negative - result, a *stressful episode*.

Critical life events versus stressful micro-episodes

The conceptualization of stressful events as episodes - i.e. the psychological reconstruction of behavior, its starting conditions, its processes and results - can be done at different levels of analysis. On a macro level, the death of a partner, for example, can be conceptualized as a stressful episode that starts with the event of the death and concludes with the end of mourning or in a more tragic way. Here the concept of 'critical life event' provides the framework. The same macro-episode can be regarded as a sequence of micro-episodes consisting, for instance, of stressful short-term episodes such as waking up at night, the emergence of painful thoughts about the separation, the distraction and tranquillisation by a sleeping pill, and going back to sleep. The stressors initiating micro-episodes can be central hassles or non-central hassles (Gruen, Folkman & Lazarus, 1988); they can vary on the dimension of their valence or 'centrality'. We postulate that macro-events can be investigated in a psychologically more pertinent way if they are analyzed at the level of micro-episodes - that is, at the level of relatively elementary behavior patterns. Molar critical life events are more easily accessible to psychological analysis when they are transposed into a sequence of more molecular micro-episodes. The sum of micro-episodes may consist of quite different and heterogenous types of coping tasks.

The structure of the micro-episodes consists of objective situation aspects which are subjectively perceived, followed by responses to this perception, and by the result of these responses.

The process of the encounter with a stressful event can be reconstructed according to stimulus-response (S-R) chains. The initial stimulus of a micro-episode is the change of a stimulus configuration in the inner or outer world (situation) of the subject. The first response consists of perceptions of change, followed by emotions as a result of an appraisal process, eventually thoughts, and finally by a coping response. The result thereof, plus perhaps further events, forms the new situation. S-R-S-R chains are thus to be based on a sequence of segmented behavioral units. The definition of the units depends on the theoretical framework.

The psychological dimensions of situations

Objective distinctive characteristics of stress

1. Loss — The removal of a desired source of reward or positive reinforcement (e.g. loss of a relationship).

2. Punishment — The occurrence of an aversive situation (e.g. an attack, road accident).

Objective dimensions of situations

1. Valence — The inherent stressfulness of a situation.

2. Controllability — The inherent opportunities for control within a situation.

3. Changeability — The probability that the situation will change by itself; that is via its own dynamics (e.g. the weather).

4. Ambiguity — The degree to which a situation is inherently lacking in sufficient information to enable clear meaning of the situation to be ascertained.

5. Reoccurrence — The inherent likelihood of reoccurrence of the stressful situation.

Since Kurt Lewin, the lack of psychological situation theories within psychology is to be deplored. Even the person-situation interaction concept, as developed within personality psychology (Pervin & Lewis, 1978; Endler & Magnusson, 1976), has not yielded a theory of situation. Rather, the problematic nature of the situation was dealt with methodologically rather than theoretically. Cognitive psychology has - in the tradition of rationalistic philosophy - incorporated the situation dimension in the cognitive dimension. It has done this primarily by granting this dimension significance as the cognitive achievement of situation interpretation.

The theories of classical and operant conditioning deal to some extent with psychologically relevant situation characteristics. This is achieved through the notions of unconditioned stimulus (UCS), conditioned stimulus (CS) and discriminative stimuli (SD), stimulus generalisation etc.. The situation has come back into focus through later theoretical developments in the psychology of control. Thus, Seligman (1975) has developed pertinent hypotheses about the psychological significance of predictability/non-predictability of aversive situations. These characteristics are analogous to those of controllability and non-controllability. The definition of these depends on the temporal position of the aversive event in the sequence of situation, reaction, and consequence. A UCS is thus defined as unpredictable if it cannot be reliably predicted by the CS in an objective way. When an organism is confronted with an unpredictable aversive UCS, a state of chronic anxiety builds up. When the UCS is predictable, a phobic reaction can be expected. If the organism has no available response for bringing about an intended consequence, this consequence is uncontrollable.

Findings from animal experiments show that aversive, uncontrollable situations - i.e. situations which cannot be terminated by reactions available to the test animal - can lead to lasting negative consequences. It can be assumed that, besides the objective non-controllability as a characteristic of the situation, the subjective perception of the situation as being non-controllable produces analogous consequences. This is regardless of its possible objective controllability. By contrast, we do not attend that the damaging effect of objectively non-controllable aversive situations can be averted by cognitive processes of illusory control. This type of inappropriate adaptation will probably have damaging effects in the long run. We are convinced that organisms with an (within certain limits) appropriate cognitive representation of the situation have a better chance of survival than organisms with distorted representations of the reality. We assume that the extent of a stressor's controllability is a psychologically relevant feature of the situation. The result of adaptive behavior will substantially depend on its matching the given controllability of the stressor. Furthermore, the stressor does not necessarily have to be located outside the organism. Internal stressors can also be described by this characteristic. Heart rate may serve as an example for the relevance of objective features of inner stressors: The heart rate can be wrongly perceived and misinterpreted as non-controllable by a person, who as a result suffers a panic attack (e.g. Ehlers, Margraf & Roth, 1988).

Proceeding from Seligman (1975), we define the objective *controllability* as the first theoretical term of our model. Objective controllability of a situation can theoretically be defined by analogy to item or task difficulty in psychological tests - interpreted as the percentage of subjects of a representative sample who are able to control the situation (i.e. produce a correct response). A consequence of high controllability is that most of a defined population are able to control the specific type of situation. It can be assessed independently of the individual as a characteristic attributed to the situation (cf. Krohne, 1990). Accordingly, a lethal illness is objectively little able to be influenced. The preparation for an exam, on the other hand, is more controllable in normal circumstances. The solution of an everyday conflict is harder to control if a sociopath rather than socially competent partner is involved. Controllability has been discussed in several studies as a coping relevant characteristic (e.g. Monat, Averill & Lazarus, 1972; Miller, 1979; McFarlane, Norman, Streiner, Roy & Scott, 1980; Folkman & Lazarus, 1980; Krohne, 1986).

A second objective characteristic of the situation is its *changeability*. By changeability we mean the objective probability of a situation changing by its own dynamics, without contribution from the person, toward the cancellation of the aversive situation or the non-arrival of an outcome involving loss. Everyone knows that choleric colleague whose angry reproaches will vanish in a short time without any intervention. This is an example of an aversive stressor of high changeability. In Scotland the changeability of the weather is obvious higher than in the Sahara.

According to the reaction-contingency model of Seligman (1975; see also Garber, Miller & Abramson, 1980), in figure 1 the x-axis represents the extent of controllability and the y-axis the extent of changeability. The figure depicts three examples of stressful situations: In *situa-*

tion A, the probability of a positive outcome is nearly the same given the best reaction. This situation is uncontrollable with a chance of about fifty-fifty percent of a positive outcome, probably eliciting reactions of both helplessness; an example for situation A would be a patient attending an operation with uncertain success. *Situation B* is uncontrollable in the same way; the chance of a positive outcome is nearly the same given the best response and given no response. But the overall chance of a positive outcome is very low, probably eliciting reactions of helplessness and hopelessness; an example for situations like B: a loud noise in a poorly insulated apartment during the night which is hardly to control. In *situation C*, the chance of positive outcome given the best response exceeds by far the changeability of the situation by its own dynamics, probably eliciting control behavior; e.g. a student preparing an important paper for classroom presentation.

Figure 1. Controllability and changeability parameters of stressful situations

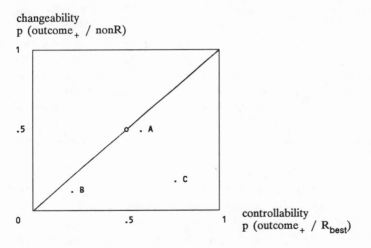

changeability
p (outcome$_+$ / nonR)

controllability
p (outcome$_+$ / R$_{best}$)

The characteristic of *ambiguity* or *intransparency* of the stressor is independent of the two above-mentioned dimensions. Aversion or loss can vary on the dimension of clarity. The certainty of the diagnosis of an illness, for instance, can be more or less pronounced. Similarly, the various implications of an event involving loss for instance can be more or less visible at a glance. Here too, the objective intransparency is to be distinguished from the subjective one. The *duration* and *temporal per-*

spective (past, present, future) of the event may be relevant time factors. Another important characteristic in this context is the *probability of reoccurrence* of the event within a certain time span.

Further relevant psychological characteristics can be classified according to the criterion of whether the stressful situation has its origin in the occurrence of an *aversive component* or in the *loss* of a positive component in the person or in the environment. In classical behavior theories, this distinction corresponds to the two types of punishment I and II (see Holland & Skinner, 1953). The two event variants evoke distinguishable psychological processes in the person, which, among other things, become visible in different emotions (see Lazarus & Smith, 1988). We will come back to this in the third section. Both aspects will also vary in severity.

A further aspect has to be taken into consideration - the possible *process aspect* of stressful events: Situations as described here don't remain necessarily sequentially static. Their characteristics such as controllability and ambiguity can change over time by their own dynamics or as a function of coping attempts. This change can constitute a new situation either partially or wholly. For example, a young boy is attacked by an older boy (situation 1) and tries to defend himself, but in so doing another boy comes and also attacks him together with the older boy (situation 2). This change reduces dramatically the controllability of the situation. Or: After a woman attempted to maintain contact with a close colleague who has moved, there is no reaction from her colleagues' side (situation 1). After some weeks and after trying again to contact her, there is still no answer (situation 2). There is a reduction in controllability for maintaining contact.

How to identify objective characteristics of situations?

There are different possibilities for identifying objective (or intersubjective) situation characteristics: the appraisal of situations (a) by experts using objective criteria and (b) by representative samples of subjects. They can be asked, for example, to what extent certain situations or events are capable of being to be influenced by certain behavior patterns. A prerequisite for both is a precise description of the events (coping tasks) and of the behavior patterns to be appraised, this being as unequivocal as possible. Finally, it is possible to induce objective situation characteristics (c) by experimental realization, as for example in the contingency experiments of Seligman and his colleagues. For further discussion see Magnusson and Stattin (1982).

Subjective perception of objective situation characteristics

The role of perception/appraisal in adaptation processes has been widely discussed by the Berkeley group (eg. Lazarus, 1966; Folkman, 1983), but also by Abramson, Seligman and Teasdale (1978), Garber, Miller and Abramson (1980) and Fisher (1986). The adaptive behavior performance is related to perceptual processes and can be predicted partly by perceptual parameters. The predictability concerns emotions as well as coping responses (Lazarus, 1982; Folkman & Lazarus, 1988).

Subjective dimensions of situations

1. Valence	The subjective meaning of a situation/ event that contributes to its stressfulness, but is individually determined.
2. Controllability	The subjective appraisal of personal ability to control the stressful situation.
3. Changeability	The subjective appraisal that the stressful event will change by itself, that is without the person any action.
4. Ambiguity	The subjective appraisal of ambiguity and uncertainty of the situation.
5. Reoccurrence	The subjective appraisal of the reoccurrence of the stressful situation.
6. Familiarity	The extent of personal experience with such a situation.

At this point, following Garber et al. (1980), the concept *subjective or perceived* probability of controllability and changeability should be introduced. Subjective controllability should be understood as a person's assessment of their ability to have a positive influence on a stressor, within a specified time span.

Another subjective situation parameter is the *valence*. Valence refers to the negative versus the positive quality of a situation in relation to its relevance (intensity) for a person. In the context of the negative events/situations that we are dealing with here, it means the extent of the subjectively appraised severity of the situation.

A further subjective situation characteristic relevant to coping is the extent of the *perceived ambiguity* of situations. This indicates the subjectively appraised degree of intransparency of a situation. The subjectively perceived location of the event in time (past, present or future) and its *duration*, as well as the perceived *probability of reoccurrence*, are also results of a person's perception of objective situation parameters. All these have implications to personal states of mind, plans and goals.

Stressful situations can change their objective psychological features as a function of coping attempts or may remain stable despite the invested efforts. They also may change by their own dynamics. This underlines the importance of subjective perceptions of such *process characteristics* during the course of stressful events. For example, the boy who is attacked first by one and then by two older boys may or may not perceive a reduction in controllability of the situation. The woman losing her colleague may or may not perceive that the loss of a good relationship is less controllable.

All the above-mentioned objective and subjective characteristics can be related to system-external or system-internal states. Accordingly, strong emotional arousal, for example, can be experienced as being of low controllability, intransparent and of high negative valence, although its origin could perhaps be clarified and the state be actively influenced.

Interindividual differences in perception tendencies

The cognitive stress theories have described self- and environment-directed processes of perception and their relation to emotions and coping reactions in a differentiated way. Along with others, we proceed from the fact that characteristics of perception influence coping responses. We furthermore assume that people differ in their (relatively stable) tendency to perceive stressors or classes of stressors as controllable, change-able, ambiguous and valent (cf. Krohne, 1990). Perceptual tendencies are also related to coping tendencies. When the perceptual tendencies rise above or fall below certain limits, we call such persons 'optimists' or 'pessimists' (cf. Fisher, 1984). 'Optimists' refers to those persons who tend to overestimate controllability and changeability of stressful events, whereas 'pessimists' tend to underestimate them. We have described and investigated the configuration of perceptual and coping characteristics for a group of depressed people (see chapters 6 and 7).

Table 1. Summary and outline of main theoretical concepts

Objective distinctive characteristics of stress

1. Loss	The removal of a desired source of reward or positive reinforcement (e.g. loss of a relationship).
2. Punishment	The occurrence of an aversive situation (e.g. an attack, road accident).

Objective dimensions of situations

1. Valence	The inherent stressfulness of a situation.
2. Controllability	The inherent opportunities for control within a situation.
3. Changeability	The probability that the situation will change by itself; that is via its own dynamics (e.g. the weather).
4. Ambiguity	The degree to which a situation is inherently lacking in sufficient information to enable clear meaning of the situation to be ascertained.
5. Reoccurrence	The inherent likelihood of reoccurrence of the stressful situation.

Subjective dimensions of situations

1. Valence	The subjective meaning of a situation/ event that contributes to its stressfulness, but is individually determined.
2. Controllability	The subjective appraisal of personal ability to control the stressful situation.
3. Changeability	The subjective appraisal that the stressful event will change by itself, that is without the person any action.
4. Ambiguity	The subjective appraisal of ambiguity and uncertainty of the situation.
5. Reoccurrence	The subjective appraisal of the reoccurrence of the stressful situation.
6. Familiarity	The extent of personal experience with such a situation.

Emotional reactions as elements of stressful episodes

Emotions are an essential component of stressful episodes. On the one hand emotional reactions are triggered and shaped by the perception/appraisal of the situation (e.g. perceived controllability of the situation) (Lazarus, Kanner & Folkman, 1980). The appraisals of situation characteristics can be analysed as *antecedent* conditions of the quality, intensity and duration of emotional reactions (e.g. Scherer, 1988; Lazarus, Coyne & Folkman, 1984). On the other hand emotions can be conceptualized as a *consequence* or outcome of efforts of regulation (e.g. Folkman & Lazarus, 1988). Some prominent conceptions of emotion and stress (Scherer, 1985; Leventhal & Scherer, 1987; Frijda, 1986) point out, that *stress* and stress-related emotions emerge if (automated) processes of emotional regulation fail to reinstall homeostasis. Then *coping behavior* is directed to the stressful situation which includes - as one important component - stress-related emotions. Such emotions may be described as 'anxiety-stress', 'depression-stress' or 'anger-stress', 'helplessness' or other negative emotional states. Coping efforts concerning emotions are called *coping with (stressful) emotions* (e.g. Laux & Weber, 1990) or *emotion-focused coping* (Lazarus & Launier, 1978). The proposed situation-behavior approach refers to this view of emotional reactions in the context of stressful situations. For this purpose we take into consideration emotional reactions or states - as characterizing the onset and the course of stressful episodes - on the following *dimensions*: 'anxious-nervous', 'depressed-sad', 'aggressive-angry', 'hesitant-inhibited', 'lethargic-indolent' and 'abandoned'. Emotions are not conceptualized as coping behavior per se, which would be another possible function of emotions in the stress and coping process (see Laux & Weber, 1991). The main interest here is to analyse processes which emerge from the appraisal of situation characteristics, i.e. the development of the episode (e.g. controllability) without special focus on different levels of information processing as discussed by other authors. Other theoretical approaches (e.g. Scherer, 1984; Leventhal & Scherer, 1987; Frijda, 1986) describe the relations of cognitive and emotional processes on different levels in a more sophisticated and more complex way.

Taxonomy of coping behavior

In the last few years, various taxonomies have been developed systematic classifications of coping behavior. Probably the best-known taxonomy
was proposed by Lazarus and Launier (1978). It systematizes the most
important types of coping with regard to their functions and to the
temporal perspective of the stressor (past, present and future). This
phenomenological taxonomy has been widely applied. On this basis, we
have developed a *theoretically oriented* taxonomy, within which the most
important coping modes are behavioral categories which form the essential criterion variables for our predictions (see below). Regardless of
whether the situation element is located within or outside a person, the
coping reactions can be directed towards changing the stressful *situation
components*. Secondly, they can aim to change the *cognitive representation*
of the stressor or - thirdly - the *orientation of volition* or *evaluation*. We
assume, like others, that the general function of the coping response is
the alleviation of the subject's discomfort and the re-establishing of
homeostasis. Subjects might choose high discomfort if this increases the
chances of obtaining long term goals.

By the *first behavior type* the inner or outer stressor is directly
intended to be changed; taking a valium or making a relaxation exercise
for calming a threatening thought are examples for instrumental behavior to cope with an *inner* stressor. An instrumental behavior to cope
with an *outer* stressor would be the attempt, for example, to calm an
angry partner in a conflict.

The *second behavior type* tends to change the cognitive representation of the situation (stressor) by suppressing or by searching for information about the situation. The search my be carried out by asking
and looking out for information in the environment or by examining memory. A person can ring up to a friend and ask him if it is true that he
criticised him yesterday in talking to another friend. The answer may
change the cognitive representation of the initial stressful element of
the situation. Or we can try to solve a particular problem in a specific
situation by recalling how we solved a similar situation previously.

The *third behavior type* is volition- and/or evaluation-oriented. We
can change our goals and intentions, what may be of higher importance
if a situation reveals as little controllable and changeable. Or we can
change our evaluation and appraisal of the stressful event by changing
our attitudes or standards.

This classification accentuates the different levels of cognitive and behavioral regulation implied in coping processes. The categories represent different functional behavior classes. The classes of this taxonomy can be split up further; for example, representation-oriented responses could be divided into 'search for information inside' vs. 'search for information outside' the person.

Figure 2. System of coping behavior with stressful episodes emerging from the environment and/or the person

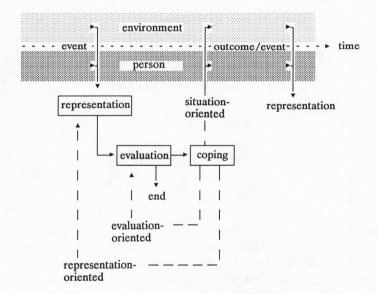

Coping operations can be divided according to their relation to the *situation components*, into active (influence the stressful component), evasive (avoiding, leaving-the-field) and passive types (omitting actions, hesitating, waiting). According to our definition of the situation they can refer to components of either the environment (e.g. to a demanding boss) or the person (e.g. to a negative cognition, to emotional arousal).

Representation-oriented coping operations are directed towards changing the cognitive representation of the situation. This can involve a search for information, but also a 'fading out', or 'suppression'. *Evaluation-* or *volition-oriented* coping operations are directed to the goal

structure or the subjective valence of the situation. This is attained by
revising the actual adaptive intentions or by changing long term goals
or standards. It also involves actual reappraisal of situation components.

Figure 3: Taxonomy of coping operations

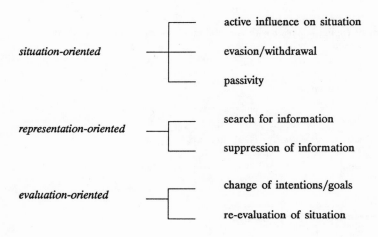

Criteria for adaptation

We understand adaptation as a sequence of reactions to an objective situation which possesses psychologically relevant features, i.e. relevant for
characteristics of the needed behavior to cope with the specific task.
The reaction begins with the subjective perception/appraisal of such situation characteristics and continues with reactions to the perceptions,
usually manifested as efforts to master the situation, when a routine or
automatic response is not available (Monat, Averill & Lazarus, 1972).
This effort is called 'coping' (see also White, 1974). The coping response
has a more or less effective influence on the initial stressor. The orga-
nism-situation adaptation should not only be evaluated by subjective
perceptions, but also by objective criteria. An analogy can be found in
the general area of experimental psychology, where the adequacy of a
test response cannot be judged solely by the subject's appraisal of
his/her performance. Rather criteria for judging performance adequacy
are based on whether the subject has sufficiently met the demands
inherent to the task.

The analysis of adaptation can focus separately on three different *correspondences:* (i) the correspondence between the subjective perception (or cognitive representation) of a given situation and the response to the subjective perception. If the responses meet the demands inherent to the characteristics of the perception/appraisal and the goals of the person, the person quickly reaches inner equilibration. In other words the response fits the subjective perception. E.g. if a person interprets a type of situation as dangerous, he or she may avoid it. If security is a goal, then this response can ensure a return to inner equilibrium in the short term. Some people suffer from an inability to act in line with their appraisals. There is an inhibition of their behavioral options. They feel angry or anxious and cannot express their emotions, and subsequentially are unable to cope as a function of their appraisals, emotions, and goals. They may experience a discrepancy between behavior performed and the perceived demands.

So far the consideration of the adaptation process concerns only inner processes and criteria. The process could be called *'inner adjustment'*. If a person succeeds in inner adjustment he or she feels equilibrated or calmed with his or her subjective standards - independently of objective features of the situation.

Figure 4. Correspondence relations between objective characteristics of the situation, subjective perception and adaptation or coping response

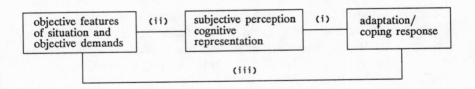

Further analyses of correspondences concern (ii) the correspondence between the subjective perception/appraisal and the objective features of the situation and (iii) the correspondence between the adaptive responses and the objective demands of the situation. The adaptive performance can be considered beyond its correspondence with the subjective perception as also matching the objective demands of the situation.

A passive reaction to a stressor that is wrongly perceived as uncontrollable may be subjectively functional, but objectively it is dysfunctional. Given the same perception, the perseveration of an instrumental control reaction would be subjectively dysfunctional but objectively functional. Adaption efforts which are objectively functional will affect the well-being of the person in the long term perspective; if they are only subjectively functional they may influence the inner short-term equilibration but probably only for a short time.

We define *objectively functional coping* as coping responses which meet the demands of the objective features of the situation. *Subjectively functional coping* is defined as coping responses which meet the demands resulting from the subjective perception of the situation.

Optimal adaptation implies - within certain limits - an adequate perception and cognitive representation of psychologically relevant situation characteristics. This short-term representation is a prerequisite of successful adaptation. If the short-term representation becomes an element of long-term memory we call it 'knowledge' (cf. Lazarus & Smith, 1988). When the situation is wrongly perceived in relation to its adaptation-relevant features, then the activation of appropriate coping reaction is less probable.

At first glance that idea seems to be in opposition to the studies of Alloy and Abramson (1979, 1982), where mildly depressed students seemed to be more 'realistic' in estimating the experienced control of lights by pressing the right button on a computer panel. There are serious problems of more than one type concerning the external validity of these findings, because the phenomenon was only produced under very specific circumstances (e.g. Brewin & Furnham, 1986): Only under non-contingency and involving no self-evaluative concerns, and only for very simple control behavior. We doubt if the results can be generalized to contexts outside the conditions of these studies. Some 'optimistic bias' of nondepressed people should fall within the limits of adequate perception (see also Beck, 1991).

Another counter argument may be the idea that 'illusion' of control may help the subject to support an unbearable reality. For example people with a lethal illness may better survive not knowing of their critical situation. There may be cases for which this particular constellation may be helpful. Nevertheless, it hardly demonstrates that the absence of the threatening information causes prolongation for survival. Lack of information at least may serve to hinder the exploitation of all available possibilities to ameliorate the physical conditions and to prolong remaining time.

Empirical research questions resulting from the theoretical assumptions

A first group of empirical research questions concern the relationship between (1) objective and (2) subjective *situation* variables with *stress emotions*. We attend, for example, that

(1) situations which objectively consist of - rather controllable - aversive stimulation by social agents are associated with more aggressive and less depressed emotions than situations consisting of - less controllable - loss and failure events;

(2) situations which are perceived as less controllable, less changeable, and as more negative valent are expected to be related with a pattern of emotions, characterized by anxious/nervous, depressed, inhibited and abandoned feelings.

A second domain of questions concerns the relationship between *perception* variables and *coping responses*. We assume that certain coping tendencies can be predicted by certain perceptual/appraisal tendencies, or that certain coping types have a functional relationship with certain types of appraisals (cf. Folkman & Lazarus, 1988; Folkman, Lazarus, Dunkel-Schetter, DeLongis & Gruen, 1986). These connections may facilitate subjective functional coping which permits inner equilibration.

On the basis of the preceding arguments, the following *central hypotheses* can be formulated and tested empirically:

(1) If controllability is perceived as high, changeability as low, and if the valence is high, an active, instrumental reaction is probable, i.e. behavior directed towards changing the stressor, be it internal or external to the system.

(2) If the changeability of the stressor is perceived as higher and similar in extent to controllability (condition of non-control according to Seligman), passivity is a likely reaction.

(3) If controllability and changeability of the stressor are perceived as low, and the valence as high, escape or evasion becomes more probable.

(4) If the subject appraises the ambiguity of the stressor as high, search for information becomes more probable; more so the higher the perceived controllability.

(5) If the stressor is perceived as transparent, and the controllability as low, suppression of information becomes more likely.

(6) In face of more short term stressors of low controllability and low valence, a re-evaluation of the situation is likely.

A third area concerns correspondences of type (ii) (see page 31): Namely to what extent is *subjective perception* influenced by *objective features* of the situation? Is correspondence associated with *mental health*? Are, for example, depressed persons characterized by a tendency to underestimate certain features of the situation (e.g. controllability or changeability)? Are there critical limits of misperception which correlate with the impairment of mental health?

Research questions concerning objectively functional coping of type (iii) deal with problems such as: Are people with the competence to meet the demands of situations with appropriate coping responses (e.g. objective controllability - instrumental behavior) more efficient in their ongoing adaptation processes than incompetent people? Are they mentally healthier than incompetent people as a long term effect?

Among the *short-term criteria* for successful adaptation are the direct solution of the problem and, on the other hand, a decrease in the stress reaction (according to rational principles, involving aspects of behavior economy, for example). *Long-term criteria* refer to physical, mental and social well-being. We therefore expect, among other things, that relevant features of mental health are correlated with the capability of appropriate cognitive representation.

According to the outline so far, *adaptation problems* can be attributed to (a) problems of perception/appraisal, e.g. due to tendencies for inadequate cognitive representation of the situation, and (b) a dysfunctional reaction to appropriate perception. This can be due to faulty, automatic habits of reacting, or lack of adequate reaction competence. These dysfunctional habits or lacking competences are to be distinguished from the subject's instrumental beliefs as to how stressors can best be coped with. The latter are representations of behavior-outcome contingencies, as they occur in the context of stressful events. Their application in the selection and regulation of behavior can be conceived in terms of individual behavior rules or instrumental beliefs (see chapter 11), especially when conscious adaptive intentions and coping actions become involved in the stressful episode.

The instrumental beliefs or behavior rules that are known to the person may be correct but not acted on by the person. In this case, it is a question of positing either dysfunctional habits or the lack of behavioral competence. Thus a distinction can be made between knowledge of what would be helpful and the skills to be able to do it. A further variant of problems consists of competing action tendencies. Also the instrumental beliefs can be dysfunctional in themselves, as for instance the opinion that controllable situations can be dealt with by withdrawing or evasion (as in a phobic avoidance).

Positively formulated, *adequate adaptation* therefore implies the following:

(1) The ability to perceive realistically the relevant characteristics of the stressor.

(2) The ability to connect the results of perception processes with functionally adequate coping reactions.

(3) As far as conscious processes are involved in selecting the reaction, to have at our disposal appropriate instrumental beliefs or behavior rules.

(4) Information about subjective and objective effectiveness of short-term coping effects; and information about long-term criteria like well-being and mental health.

In the following chapters the theoretical framework and the assumptions are subject to new methodological developments and they are tested in several empirical studies in different areas of health psychology.

Part II of the book, *New approaches to the assessment*, deals with the development of two new methods; a process-based stimulus-response questionnaire and a computer-assisted self-observation method. Both methods are applied empirically in order to test their validity within the proposed theoretical framework.

Part III, *Applications in clinical and health psychology*, presents different contributions studying the application of the situation-behavior approach - and the instruments developed - in different domains of stress and coping behavior: people suffering from depression, people suffering from a somatic disease implying severe psychological problems (HIV-infection), stress, coping and psychological health in 'normal' people, and work stress of people in an institution. Finally, we present a behavior rule approach which seeks to conceptualize and to assess appropriate coping within the situation-behavior framework. The conclusion tries to evaluate the results in line with the theory.

But first of all, there are *Harry and Evelyn* again. Their case studies may illustrate the main ideas of the theoretical outline in everyday stressful situations.

Case studies II: Theoretical analysis of the episodes

The two case studies are analysed below in terms of the theoretical framework described previously.

Harry is lost

Harry experienced a stressful situation. The stream of behavior was interrupted when he noticed that he was lost and realized that he would be late. This disturbed his inner homeostasis.

Important objective properties of the situation were: the lack of time, a low probability that the problem would be solved in absence of an instrumental influence by Harry (= low changeability) and a moderate probability of succeeding by asking for help (moderate controllability). The aversive situation is to some extent characterised by its uncertainty. Arriving too late would risk jeopardizing his chances of gaining the employment. Furthermore, the street is small, hard to find and unknown to many people.

The *subjective perception of the situation* was: Harry perceived the situation correctly concerning the remaining time and the low changeability. The situation was important for him (high valence), knowing that being late could negatively influence the director. Most important was his conviction that he could succeed, if he made an active attempt to get help from others. His subjective opinion on the controllability of the situation - 'Lets try - I'll still have a chance of finding help!' - was a necessary condition for mastering the troublesome situation. A depressive person would expect to have no chance of solving a similar problem. He would underestimate controllability, i.e. think 'here is nothing I can do'.

How did Harry cope? His perception of the situation disposed him at first to gain more information. As this representation-oriented coping alone was not successful, he continued with an attempt to influence his social environment by asking for help. An instrumental coping attempt was an appropriate, adaptive response to a situation with moderate controllability and low changeability.

Evelyn has lost her earring

The stressful situation in the second episode consists of the loss of a loved object. The *micro-episode begins* with Evelyn's awareness of her predicament. If the emotional arousal was gradually rising in the first example, so it was increased in the second.

The *objective features of the situation* are characterised by an extremely unlikely probability of finding the lost earring, with or without a careful search. Both probabilities, changeability and controllability, are very low. Her *subjective perception* of the situation corresponds more or less to the objective conditions. She soon recognizes that it is a waste of time looking for the lost earring.

How did she cope with the loss? Her low changeability and controllability expectation disposed her to adapt to the circumstances by re-evaluation and by an initial attempt at an attitude change. The representation-oriented coping attempt is connected with situation-oriented instrumental aspects. Some of her self-instructions may contain a palliative effort to calm her emotions (inner situation), and she informed the owner of the golf-course of this unfortunate incident, which represents a situation-oriented coping response (outer situation). However, changing her attitude was her decisive adapting response with regard to our theoretical framework. The stressor was neither controllable, nor was it to be expected that the problem would be solved by its own dynamic. The appropriate answer to this coping task is a evaluation-oriented coping response.

PART II

METHODS:

NEW APPROACHES TO THE ASSESSMENT
OF STRESS AND COPING

2. A stimulus-response process questionnaire

Michael Reicherts

Basic aims and procedures

The *'Stress and Coping Process Questionnaire'* (SCPQ; 'Umgang mit Bela-stungen im Verlauf (UBV)' in German; Reicherts & Perrez, 1991; Per-rez & Reicherts, 1987a) was developed to measure the variables of the theoretical approach outlined above. The basic aim of the questionnaire is to look at different dimensions of the way in which a person deals with specific stressful episodes in their daily life with respect to hypothetically relevant parameters. The assessment will be made at several points in time, corresponding to different stages of the stressful episodes. Its goal is to partly represent the transactional character and processes of stress and coping.

The process of coping should be assessed, on the one hand, by measuring it several times in the course of an episode and, on the other hand, by comparing episodes that are similar to each other in important objective characteristics. The episodes represent examples of a class or type of stressful situations so that the responses can be aggregated as reaction tendencies representative of these types of situations. The re-action is analysed as a composite of behavior with cognitive, behavioral and emotional elements. Central to this is the coping action or behavior which is preceded by the subject's appraisal of the situation and proces-ses of goal formation after the disturbance of homeostasis.

More specifically, the instrument will record the following aspects of coping:
(1) perception/appraisal of the situation characteristics
(2) emotional reactions
(3) goals of the coping process
(4) coping actions or behaviors
      (4.1) self-directed, mostly intrapsychic
      (4.2) environment-directed

(5) evaluation of the consequences (outcome)
(6) causal attribution of final outcome.

The process, which seeks to model behavior in stressful situations, is
organized structurally and sequentially, as in the TOTE concept (Miller
et al., 1960; see also the 'stress event cycle' of McGrath, 1982; or
Fisher, 1984). A stressful episode is seen as being composed of several
phases or cycles, each of which is regarded as a situation-behavior-
outcome unit. Each consecutive phase begins with the consequences of
the coping action as a continued, but widely unchanged situation. The
episode ends with a positive or negative final situation, the outcome of
the stress and coping sequence. The outcome is then to be evaluated
and attributed to causal factors. The sequence is conceptualized as the
chaining of several stimulus-response units (see figure 5). Therefore,
referring to the so-called stimulus-response (S-R) inventories (e.g.
Endler, Hunt & Rosenstein, 1962; Endler & Okada, 1975), it is here
referred to as a *S-R-S-R process questionnaire*.
        The development of the stimulus material - the standardized
stressful episodes - was based on the principles and procedures elaborated within the criterion-referenced approach of measurement (Ebel,
1962; Glaser, 1963; Lord & Novick, 1968; Klauer, 1987). It was
important that the content validity (Klauer, 1984) and content
representativeness (Wieberg, 1983) of the test tasks were established as
far as possible. Therefore, situation and behavioral aspects had to be
structured separately at first. The construction and evaluation was done
as objectively as possible. Hence, new procedures were taken in several
respects:
        The various event characteristics (controllability, changeability,
valence, ambiguity, domain or theme) were transposed into narrative stimulus material and prototypical stressful episodes were construed. The
single episodes, furthermore had to be comparable in important aspects.
Special problems here involved were the multioperational and multidimensional aspects of the assessment over time (sequential structure). A
start was made in solving this complex construction problem, although
the results of the rational strategy of construction was not entirely
satisfactory in all cases. Preliminary forms of the stimulus-construction
and the operationalization of the different variables of the response
component were elaborated and evaluated in an extensive pilot study.
In this study, the questionnaire about 'Coping with stressful situations by
adolescents' ('BS-J'; Reicherts, 1986) was developed. This was only a

one-step stimulus-response inventory assessing the same variables of appraisal and coping. It was tested in two separate studies, involving 135 and 425 adolescents respectively (Reicherts, 1986; Perrez & Reicherts, 1987a; Ulrich, 1987). On the whole, this S-R questionnaire yielded encouraging results as to reliability, construct validity and external validity (mental health).

Figure 5. The situation-behavior process in the S-R-S-R task of the SCPQ research version (example: episode of loss with positive outcome)

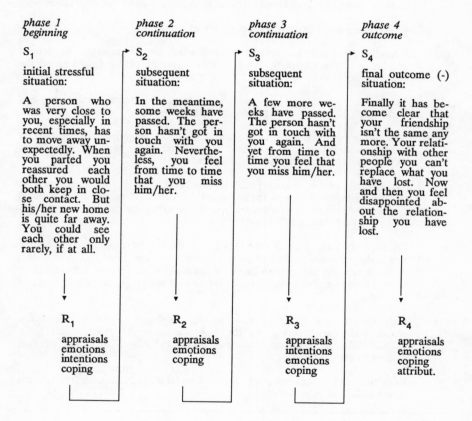

phase 1 beginning	phase 2 continuation	phase 3 continuation	phase 4 outcome
S_1	S_2	S_3	S_4
initial stressful situation:	subsequent situation:	subsequent situation:	final outcome (-) situation:
A person who was very close to you, especially in recent times, has to move away unexpectedly. When you parted you reassured each other you would both keep in close contact. But his/her new home is quite far away. You could see each other only rarely, if at all.	In the meantime, some weeks have passed. The person hasn't got in touch with you again. Nevertheless, you feel from time to time that you miss him/her.	A few more weeks have passed. The person hasn't got in touch with you again. And yet from time to time you feel that you miss him/her.	Finally it has become clear that your friendship isn't the same any more. Your relationship with other people you can't replace what you have lost. Now and then you feel disappointed about the relationship you have lost.
R_1	R_2	R_3	R_4
appraisals emotions intentions coping	appraisals emotions coping	appraisals intentions emotions coping	appraisals emotions coping attribut.

The development of the episodic items in the process questionnaire took place in the following steps (see table 2). The authors of the book and a further researcher were responsible for developing the stimulus materials. The expert ratings were carried out by 5 independent experts, all of them clinical psychologists with practical experience. The procedures used in developing each item (i.e. the single test episode) were therefore many.

Table 2. Steps of the construction of the S-R-S-R questionnaire (SCPQ research version)

(1) Conceptualization of
(1.1) the situation components (stressful events),
(1.2) the behavioral components (cognitive, emotional and behavioral responses), and
(1.3) the sequence (type of episodes, type of process);

(2) Definition of classes of tasks or subtests which are characterized by defined properties of the situations, the sequential structure of the episodes and the domain.

(3) Development of item schemata, propositional structure, definitions and dictionaries, also for the single phases of the episodes.

(4) Conception of initial situations (about 100 'plots') varying as to the type of stress, actuality (factual or potential), domain and source of stress; selection of 64 items with an even mixture (initial phases or starting events).

(5) Expert-rating of the characteristics of construction, of the appropriateness of the coping behavior and of the supposed diagnostic relevance of the stressful events for depressive behavior; analysis of the expert-ratings per item using a kind of concordance coefficient

(6) Selection of 6 items/episodes for each type of stressor after successive evaluation and selection; consideration of some parallel items for social and professional domains; revision and standardization of the initial phases; preparation of a short version for the study of depression in the clinical setting (altogether 10 items or episodes).

(7) Development of the stimulus material for the complete test episodes (consecutive phases and final situation) by the task schemata, the propositional form, characteristics and parameters of construction and adaptation to the different content of the situation.

(8) Examination of concordance with the task patterns, reformulation and revision of the classes of situations.

The construction of the stimulus material

The structuring of the stimulus material proceeded from a systematic evaluation of the characteristics of the type of event, its domain, its actuality, and the source of stress, as shown in table 4. Ambiguity of the aversive stimulation was considered an additional factor in type of stress, therefore some of the aversive stimulus episodes should present a rather ambiguous stressful event. The development of the items was based on propositional structures, as shown in table 3.

The 'dictionary' in table 3 contains definitions, examples and semantic units which can be inserted as qualitative variables into the propositional structure. Four phases underlie the structuring of the process (course of the episodes), a fourth of which, the final situation, consists of two different outcomes or results. The first phases describe lasting or ongoing and stressful events.

The *course of the episodes* proceeded from the following types:

(1) *loss and failure*: Loss is looming at the beginning (phase 1; fig. 5), and becomes virtually unavoidable or imminent during the course of the episode (phase 2 and 3; fig. 5), i.e. there remains only a very small probability that the loss or failure will not occur. Although the positive outcome (phase 4; fig. 5) depicts the final loss, a substitute reinforcement has been found; the negative outcome also depicts the final loss yet without successful substitution of reinforcement.

(2) *aversive stimulation* (including ambiguous aversive situations): The aversive stimulus at the beginning (phase 1) continues or is reinforced (phase 2 to phase 3). The positive outcome of phase 4 contains the successful cancellation/removal of the source of stress; the negative one the continuation of stress.

For the construction of the aversive stimulus type of episode, the propositional form outlined in table 3 was used.

The rules of constructing the stimuli, the form of evaluation and the task patterns (i.e. the basic propositional structure and the parameters of construction) - form a heuristic method for rule guided task construction, which is to be as transparent and intersubjective as possible. The instructions and descriptions of the situations were presented in the second person (polite form in German) and the present tense.

Participants were asked to vividly imagine the events and to remember similar events which they had experienced. The response items, in contrast, are formulated in the first person, propositional form.

Table 3. Components for the standardized construction of stressful stimulus episodes

---

propositional form for the *process* of stressful episodes *(aversive situations)*

phase 1   An /AVERSIVE STIMULATION/ (class of stressor)
             /OCCURS/ (actuality)

phase 2   /MINUTES/ or /HOURS/ pass (time span)
             and a stressor of (comparative characteristics)
             /EQUAL/ class, /IDENTICAL/ or /SIMILAR/ source, /EQUAL/ domain
             /OCCURS/ or /CONTINUES/ again

phase 3   /MINUTES/ or /HOURS/ pass
             and a stressor of
             /EQUAL/ class, /IDENTICAL/ or /SIMILAR/ source, /EQUAL/ domain
             /OCCURS/ or /CONTINUES/ again

phase 4   /MINUTES/ or /HOURS/ pass
(outcome)   and the stressor /CHANGES/ to the better (positive outcome)
             or the stressor /REMAINS UNCHANGED/ (negative outcome)

---

combination of propositional form, situation parameters and dictionary *(situation of loss)*

propositional form   A /LOSS/ (class of stressor)
                      of a /CLOSE PERSON/ (source of stress)
                      in the /SOCIAL CONTEXT/ (domain)
                      is /IMPENDING/ (actuality)

situation   controllability = /average to low/
parameters   changeability = /low/
                      valence = /average to high/
                      ambiguity = /low/

dictionary (extract) /LOSS/ is the long term or final removal of important, close per-
                      sons, loved things (pets or objects), job, certain professional tasks,
                      important arrangement or plans.
                      The /LOSS/ of a /PERSON/ can be due to his or her death, mo-
                      ving away, or termination of the relationship
                      A /CLOSE PERSON/ is a person to whom contact and exchange
                      is comparatively open, intensive, continuous.
                      In the /SOCIAL CONTEXT/ a /CLOSE PERSON/ is the partner, a
                      close relative and friend, or a good neighbour; in the
                      /PROFESSIONAL CONTEXT/ he or she is a good colleague or co-
                      worker.
                      A /LOSS/ is /IMPENDING/ when events occur which lead probab-
                      ly to a loss or which indicate its occurrence; also when a tempo-
                      rary loss occurs that isn't definitive yet but might persist.

The 10 episodes used in the study of depressive people (see chapters 6 and 7) are as follows:

Aversive and ambiguous situations:
criticism from the partner
criticism from a colleague
argument about problems in a relationship
being charged with a difficult job by the boss
reproaches by acquaintances about lacking commitment
reproaches from colleagues about professional commitment

Situations of loss and failure:
loss of a friendly relationship (a close person moves away)
loss of a loyal and cooperative work relationship (a colleague leaves)
failure of a weekend arrangement (a trip to visit someone fails)
failure of an interesting side job (a side job doesn't work out)

Table 4. Characteristics of the stimulus episodes in the SCPQ

type of stressor	actuality	domain	source	
aversive stimulation	occurs	social	close acquainted strange	persons
		professional	work activity equal superior	persons
loss and failure	impends then occurs	social	persons activities/projects objects	
		professional	persons activities/projects objects	

The two prototypes of aversive stimulation and or loss/failure represent patterns with a set of characteristics which can vary within defined ranges while other aspects can be freely shaped (see tables 3 and 4). The developed episodes (structurally identical and similar in character)

are to be considered as examples of these two prototypes. They form complex stimuli of two subtests. The prototype (defined here by propositional structure, parameter, type of episode and rules of construction) is the 'mould' of the items on the respective subtest.

In short, the two prototypes can be described by means of the characteristics suggested in chapter 1. Loss or failure depicts a more complex event with a greater time span (days up to weeks), where the stressful event is impending at the beginning. This event is on the whole less controllable, less changeable and rather transparent (with little ambiguity). The related coping actions are to a higher extent molar: cognitive re-evaluation and instrumental reorientation (substitution of reinforcers) are especially appropriate attempts which should increase as the stressful event becomes definite. Palliation is less likely to be molecular, directed towards acute and action impairing emotions as the case for aversive prototypes.

The prototype of aversive stimulation depicts somewhat less complex, more short term events of a duration of a few minutes up to a few hours, with stress that has already occurred. It is definite (or ambiguous), more controllable and somewhat more changeable than the prototype for loss or failure. The related coping actions are more molecular, eg. demanding immediate, assertive responses often with a social vis-a-vis, higher and lasting attention (search for information) and less suppression of information as well as a quicker re-evaluation in the sense of a change of immediate intentions and not of long term goals or values, as is the case for losses.

When the aversive stimulation lasts or recurs, the impending losses become increasingly concrete, to a point where they definitely occur. Thus, in spite of lasting stress in both forms, different aspects of development are indicated. It was evident that the formation of these prototypes should be considered as an experiment. The prototypes would have to stand up to empirical testing in the form of analysis of questionnaire responses from different samples (see for example chapter 3).

The construction of the response component

The conceptualization of the response-component of coping with stress for the single test tasks followed the behavioral concepts as developed earlier in this text. Understandably, in the responses to the questionnaire, only some of the variables could be explicitly transposed. The

The items were presented in propositional form and not as a question. Basically, with a few exceptions, two types of scales were used. For scaled answers, 6-point Likert-scales were used, as shown below. The scales do not have a defined middle and therefore force a choice to one side of the scale.

0	1	2	3	4	5
very small	small	rather small	rather large	large	very large

For the answers related to the coping activities, the subjective probability is assessed along a 5-point scale, with the probability levels marked as follows:

0	1	2	3	4
not at all	hardly	perhaps	probably	certainly
0%	25%	50%	75%	100%

Emotional reactions

The assessment of emotional reactions to stressful events is based on self reports of probable emotional reactions to the imagined, potentially stressful situations. Probable emotional reactions were rated on three aspects/dimensions: (1) anxious/nervous vs. composed/calm, (2) depressed/sad vs. cheerful/serene and (3) angry/furious vs. gentle/peaceful. These three experiential dimensions of experience are plausible for all stimulus-situations, even if they record relevant stress related emotions only in part (see the additional scales in COMRES; chapter 4). They were constructed on the basis of the most highly loaded items of a emotionality inventory (EMI situative; Ullrich & Ullrich, 1978) and formulated as bipolar rating scales.

Appraisals of the situation

Changeability, controllability, valence and familiarity were also registered on the basis of the items which were found to be reliable in the BS-J. The appraisal of the situations was operationalized as follows:

(1) belief in changeability: 'The chances of this situation taking

(1) belief in changeability: 'The chances of this situation taking a turn for the better without effort on my part are ... ' (very small---very large);

(2) belief in controllability: 'The chances that I can influence this situation for the better are ...' (very small---very large);

(3) negative valence: 'The overall amount of stress for me in this situation is ...' (very small---very large);

(4) familiarity: 'I have experienced a similar situation ... (never before---very often).

Except for familiarity appraisals of the situation are asked for at the beginning and continuation of the presented episode.

Coping goals and intentions

The coping intentions were weighted according to their subjective relevance (6-point scales, as above, bipolar), in propositional form: 'In this situation my intentions are as follows ... ' (not important at all---very important).

The goal dimensions used were based upon a theoretical considerations (see also Weber & Laux, 1990): The first goal was concerned with the person-environment-adaptation whereby on the one hand (1.1) the *alloplastic* adaptation of the stressful environment to the person was assessed, and on the other hand (1.2) the *autoplastic* adaptation of the person to the stressful environment. *Alloplastic* adaptation means, that the person makes an attempt to change the environment in order to reduce the stressfulness of the situations, whereas *autoplastic* adaptation refers to the attempt to accommodate oneself to the situation. These two forms had to be specified in view of the two types of stressors: In situations of loss and failure (1.1) corresponds to the goal to prevent loss or failure (or to regain the source of reinforcement) and (1.2) to the substitutive goal to gain new sources of reinforcement or to substitute the lost ones. In aversive episodes the alloplastic intention corresponds to the self asserting impact on the source of stress and the autoplastic to the keeping of the social balance, of the friendly atmosphere etc. For the goal dimensions, (2) *emotional equilibration* and (3) *self-esteem equilibration*, it was not necessary to match the operationalization to the different types of stress. For the goals, (1.1) and (1.2), the formulation of the intentions - as well as the types of stress - had to be adapted to the specifics of the situation.

Examples: For loss, the intentions are
(1.1) alloplastic person-environment-adaptation: 'To maintain a good relationship to this person ...',
(1.2) autoplastic person-environment-adaptation: 'To find satisfactory relationships with others ...',
(2) emotional equilibration: 'To remain calm and composed ...',
(3) self-esteem equilibration: 'To keep my self-esteem ...'.

The distinction between (1) and (2) can partly be compared to the distinction between problem and emotion focused coping as made by Lazarus (see Lazarus & Launier, 1978). In the transparent aversive situations in (1.1) the active intention to influence the situation by abolishing or reducing the aversive stimulation (stressor) is in the foreground, in the more ambiguous aversive situations the intention is active instrumental clarification of what the stress is about. Both are, at least partly, in conflict with the intention (1.2): in the aversive situations where the stress is socially based, autoplastic intention is concerned with the upkeep of a friendly atmosphere and the prevention of an argument with the stressful other person and thus indirectly with not being socially rejected (social desirability).

Coping behavior

The conceptualization of the behavioral aspect of the coping attempts is based on the taxonomy of behavior dimensions that is related to the situation, representation and evaluation. A selection was necessary here. The presentation proceeds from the basis that the person subjectively scales certain coping variants - *operators* - according to the probability of actually reproducing them in the face of the described hypothetical situation. In the presentation two types of coping, self-directed and environment-directed, are distinguished.

The group of *self-directed coping* consists of cognitive and intrapsychic responses:
(1) *Search for information* (internally): by focusing attention, visualizing, clarifying, remembering etc. According to the type of stressful situation used here, the search for information can be directed to stress-

ful events and states as well as to conditions of the person, such as possibilities for action or well-being.

(2) *Suppression of information:* by withdrawing attention, fading out, looking for a distraction. This intrapsychic coping response, too, can be applied to information (cues etc.) about the stressful event as well as to the shortcomings or restrictions of one's own possibilities for action. This doesn't need to be mentioned in the formulation of the items.

(3) *Re-evaluation:* changing the evaluations by relating them to personal or interpersonal comparison, by accepting, resigning or by finding a new view on things.

(4) *Palliation:* palliative ways of behavior aimed at the (direct) smoothing of stress emotions, by cognitive activity (calming self-instructions) as well as by instrumental palliative actions ('discharge') such as smoking, drug taking (psychotropic substances), eating or drinking. Examples of items for this complex type of coping are given in brackets above and show the different variants of palliation. The preferences are differentiated using questions in a 9-item supplementary rating at the end of the process questionnaire (see appendix).

The functional behavior classes are outlined in the basic model in chapter 1. Whilst (1) and (2) aim at modifying the representation of the actual situation, (3) is directed towards a change in the (first) evaluation of the present situation, or to the standards or values themselves. Palliation (4) is a situation-directed coping action which tries to influence the stress related states of the subject, namely the affective states. It can take place wholly internally, but can also instrumentally interfere with the environment (e.g. by taking a medicine). When depressive or anxious coping strategies to stress take place, a further dimension of self-directed internal activities is possible, namely the cognitive activities of taking responsibility, blaming or reproaching someone for the occurred event with intrapunitive or extrapunitive character:

(5) *Self-blame* or intrapunitive, cognitive behavior: internal activities of self-blame, self-critic, self-pity. This can occur to a lesser degree, e.g. as taking responsibility, or to a higher degree such as self-punishment by autoaggressive phantasies.

(6) *Blame of others* or extrapunitive cognitive behavior: aggressive accusation of others, blaming other people, or the circumstances, reproaching of others etc., that are cradled inwardly, and not expressed or made visible outwardly. The overt expression of blaming, anger for

example, which may be instrumental can be reported in the environment-directed coping responses (see below).

These six functional behavior classes of self-directed coping strategies are identically applied to the different types of stress (aversive ambiguous events and events of loss and failure) and to the different phases of the episodes (except the outcome phase). They cover different facets, but are not exhaustive.

The second group is formed by the *environment-directed, instrumental coping* attempts, represented by a question of their own. They were to be presented differently for the different types of stress and are outlined below:

(1) Environment-directed coping strategies in *aversive and ambiguous* situations:

(1.1) Active, instrumental impact on the stressor by attempts to influence or to confront the other person; in situations which are not transparent by active-assertive investigation on the source of the ambiguity in order to clarify it (by questioning, asking for clarification etc.);

(1.2) evasive behavior: avoiding or withdrawing;

(1.3) passive behavior: hesitating, waiting or resigning;

(2) Environment-directed coping behavior in situations of *loss and failure*:

(2.1) Activities to prevent impending loss or failure, to prevent or - if only transitory - abolish or cancel loss or failure,

(2.2) Activities to re-orientate, to make substitute sources of reinforcement, to (re)gain equivalent reinforcers.

(2.3) passive behavior: waiting, hesitating or resigning.

These functional classes of environment-directed, instrumentally relevant coping behavior are - except for the adaptation to the sequence (see below) and some variants of the formulation - similarly presented for all three phases of the episodes.

As to the psychological meaning of the descriptions of the strategies, it has to be pointed out that some variants can probably express different things in the course of an episode: at the start of an episode of loss, with a possible loss looming, 'to remain passive' can be of a waiting character rather than where the loss is virtually a fact at the end of an episode and where 'to remain passive' tends to imply resigning or giving up.

Causal attributions

The assessment of the causal attribution regarding the positive or negative outcome of the stressful episodes was done at the end, for the positive or negative outcome of the episode as a whole. The supposed causes were rated by the subject him/herself according to the following dimensions (see Weiner, 1982; Abramson et al., 1979; Hammen & Cochran, 1981): (1) internal-external, (2) global-specific and (3) stable-variable. It asked for a scaling to record whether the supposed causes (which are not made explicit) were proportionally more or less within one's own self or if they were located in the other participants or within the circumstances. An attempt was made to develop 6-point scales with two poles for each dimension of the causal attributions, with scale steps that force a decision as no mid-point of the scale was envisaged.

Expert-ratings and selection of the situations

In the expert-rating, which was independently conducted by five experienced clinical psychologists, the predominant category (modus) or the central tendency (median or arithmetic means) of the expert judgement was registered for each item. The concordance of the judgements for each item was also calculated, either absolutely (for the categorical judgements) or as the proportion of the judgement-variance per maximum variance possible, according to the formula (Fricke, 1974; see also Lienert, 1978):

$$C = 1 - \frac{\text{sums of squares of the judgement values}}{\text{maximum possible sums of squares of the judgements}}$$

For a situation to be considered, a concordance of $C = .80$ (i.e. 80%) minimum *for all* categories of judgements (the construction characteristics 'type of stress', 'actuality', 'domain' and 'social distance') was required; and $C > = .67$ (i.e. a maximum absolute error of a third of the variance of judgements possible) in the 6-point scale judgements *for all* of the other parameters which are ambiguity, changeability, controllability and general valence was necessary. So the examination of content validity concentrated on the single episode by means of several criteria.

The experts also assessed the diagnostic relevance, the probability of a depressed person experiencing such an event and the probability that he/she would show an appropriate coping behavior in a similar situation (6-point scales). With C=.97 (controllability and changeability) and C=.91 (ambiguity and valence), the average concordance of the experts for the construction parameters can be described as good. The variance of the ratings was less than 10% of the max. possible variance. The average extent of the valence and the diagnostic relevance can also be considered satisfactory.

It is understood that with so many construction characteristics there are always single test tasks with an erratic and unsatisfactory value. We have accepted such cases in the hope that the content validity of the tasks is preserved overall. The content validity of the episodes chosen for the clinical study seems satisfactory.

Revision and the construction of the final version

After the test analysis in a sample of normal adults (N=65), this research version of the S-R-S-R process questionnaire was applied in a clinical study, which is reported in chapters 6 and 7. The results were used to modify the instrument and to prepare a final version which could be standardized (stanine norms) and prepared for diagnostical application.

The criteria for the selection of items or entire episodes for the *final version* of the SCPQ (Reicherts & Perrez, 1991; see appendix), were (1) balancing the underlying stressor taxonomy and (2) optimizing the response characteristics of *all* response variables, i.e. item difficulty and item-scale correlations (in a weighted criterium).

The final version of the questionnaire contains 18 episodes (from the basic pool of 36 episodes), and for reasons of economy presents only three phases of the stressful episodes instead of the four phases of the research version (phase 2 of the original version was eliminated). Each response variable is presented in one standard formulation, and there were also slight changes in formulation of the rating response (e.g. subjective probability is estimated without percentage levels of probability). Also the causal attribution dimensions were changed to make them easier to handle (one rating asks for the degree of internal causes, one rating for external causes due to the other person(s), and one rating for external causes due to the circumstances).

The final version yielded highly satisfactory reliability coefficients: split-half reliability and Cronbach Alpha (N=100 normal adult subjects) varied from $r_{tt}=.71$ to $r_{tt}=.95$ depending on the variables (median of $r_{tt}=.87$). Retest-reliability involved administering a shortened-version after 6 weeks (N=30), and varied from $r_{tt}=.64$ to $r_{tt}=.91$ (median of $r_{tt}=.80$).

The questionnaire also gave a satisfactory predictive validity predicting stress and coping behavior in the natural setting of N=60 students recorded via self-observation (see chapter 5, reliability and validity paragraph). The test material of the final version is presented in appendix.

The construction rationale of SCPQ was successfully applied to develop similar stimulus-response questionnaires containing different stressful situations: For people with HIV-infection and AIDS (see chapter 8), for adolescents (Reicherts, 1986), and also for stressful interactions of the mother and her baby (Reicherts, Schedle & Diethelm, 1989).

3. The impact of situation and process on stress and coping

Michael Reicherts & Meinrad Perrez

Problem

In this chapter some of the effects of type of situation, the process of stressful encounters and their interaction on appraisal, emotion and coping are analysed. The analysis is conducted using the theoretical assumptions described in chapter 1. The results can be interpreted as a contribution to theoretical or construct validity of the S-R-S-R process questionnaire method described in chapter 2.

Previous work in personality psychology from a situationist perspective has shown situations to be an important determinant of behavior. Magnusson, Endler, Mischel, Epstein, Bem and others have made an essential contribution to the study of situation determinants of behavior.

With the risk of oversimplification, there are at least four distinguishable positions concerning the impact of situations in the context of explanation and prediction of behavior:

(1) the classic *'personalist'* position (or 'dispositionism') is characterised by supposing broad and stable traits of the person which determine his/her behavior; different reformulations of the traditional trait conception have been proposed (cf. Laux & Vossel, 1982);

(2) the *'situationist'* position postulates the actual situation factors or constellations as having the greatest influence in determining the persons' behavior (e.g. Mischel, 1968; here classical behavioristic approaches are also apparent);

(3) the *'social learning'* position emphasizes the importance of cognitive processes. The impact of situation is mediated by the subject's interpretation of the situation. Different intervening factors, such as perception, expectancies, goals etc. have been described by Mischel (1973) and others.

(4) the *interactionist'* position considers behavior to be a product of a special (not a statistical) reciprocal effect of personality and situation factors (e.g. Endler & Magnusson, 1976; Ekehammar, 1974; Magnusson, 1980).

Conceptualisation of stress and coping behavior by Lazarus and co-workers which is based on a *transactional perspective* also focuses on interaction in a somewhat broadened, process-oriented view. They also emphasize the role of cognitive processes. But assessing stress and coping processes without identifying any tendency on the part of the individual to behave in defined types of situation doesn't help much to explain and predict behavior, as mentioned by Krohne (1990; see also Lazarus, 1990). McCrae (1989) showed that coping dispositions (traits) and their interaction with the type of stressful situation explained statistically more variance than situation determinants by their own. He emphasizes that different types of coping behavior are more or less specific to different stressful situations.

There is, to some extent, agreement that the strength of situation properties may be a critical aspect with regard to its impact: the stronger certain (objective) properties are, such as aversiveness, the stronger the impact of the situation on behavior. For most individuals stressful situations seem to constitute a rather 'strong' situation class, which is not homogeneous (i.e. there are different subclasses), but their dispositions or tendencies to feel and to behave are nevertheless of great importance.

The intention in this chapter, however, is not to demonstrate the dominance of situation effects over the influence of trait personality factors, but rather to show the influence of specific situation effects on appraisal and coping behavior with regard to situation- and process specific tendencies, especially to coping behavior dispositions. We argue for a position between the global 'traitist' and the singular 'encounterist' position, which only accepts single but constantly changing processes without regularity and stability.

The situation-behavior approach at first refers to the *inter-action* between the situation and the person. But there are different situations (e.g. described by *characteristics* such as controllability and by particular *phases* of the process such as beginning of an episode) 'producing' specific stress and coping behavior; and there are also differences between subjects behaving according to their different tendencies to appraise, to feel and to cope. The aim of the following chapter is to describe and to analyse the relationship between situation determinants, their perception by the subject, the phase of the process and the subject's behavior. The exact proportion of variance explained by the situation, the person, or their interaction is not of interest. Rather the initial intention is to explain and predict behavior by relying on specific determinants of the situation. The person's determinants are analysed via *tendencies of appraisal* of the objective situations, and of *tendencies* of stress and coping behavior.

Hypotheses

Hypotheses are formulated according to the variables represented in and measured by the questionnaire (in chapter 2; see also chapter 1, predictions).

(1) Effects of situation and process characteristics on *subjective appraisals* and on *emotional reactions* of a stressful episode:

(1.1) According to the objectives of the construction, subjects should perceive higher controllability and changeability in the aversive episodes than in the loss or failure episodes.

(1.2) In both types of stressful situations controllability and changeability should be perceived as lower over the course of the episodes, from phase 1 to phase 2, due to the stressor remaining unchanged over time.

(1.3) Negative valence should be similarly perceived in the two subtests, but should be increased in the course of the (unchanged) stressful episodes. There should be a strong difference between positive and negative outcome as described in the hypothetical end of the episode (phase 3).

(1.4) Concerning the theme or content of the two classes of stressful episodes, it is to be supposed that aversive stimulation by social agents (as presented in some episodes) produces more aggressive and less depressed emotions than the looming loss or failure events.

(2) Effects of situation and process on *situation-directed* behavior:

(2.1) The less controllable the situations (gross and net control) the less active influence on the stressor will be exerted by the subject and

(2.2) the more passivity (hesitation or resignation) will occur.

(3) Effects on *representation-directed* coping efforts: The lower the ambiguity of the stressful situation then

(3.1) the more limited the search for information, and

(3.2) the more the subject will suppress information about the stressor.

(4) *Evaluation-directed* coping efforts: The less controllable the situation,

(4.1) the more the instrumental goals (of influence, substitution) are changed from more alloplastic to more autoplastic adaptation, especially when stressful effects are long-lasting; because social aversive stressors as conceived in the SCPQ episodes probably represent a stronger attack on the self-esteem of the subject, his or her coping intentions should focus more on the goal of (re)equilibration of self-esteem;

(4.2) the more re-evaluation is increased to change the relevance or valence of the actual situation.

Method

The final version of the S-R-S-R process questionnaire (SCPQ) was used (see chapter 2 and appendix). The 9 responses of each subtest - aversive situations vs. loss/failure - within each phase were aggregated using mean scores. This procedure is possible since distributions are normal, and consistency of the episodes in both subtests and correlations between phases 1 and 2 are strong enough. These four values per variable are analysed using a 2x2 or 2x4 repeated measures design, with situation and process as within-group factors. Analyses are conducted in SAS GLM procedure.

Subjects

A sample of 100 non-student adults, 51 women and 49 men - mean age 38 years (std 11.8) - answered the questionnaire. As regards their level of formal education, 22% left after elementary school, 38% were of professional skilled status, 19% left after high school and 21% were university graduates. About 50% of them were married.

Results

Appraisals of the situation (see table 5)

There were strong effects of type of situation ($F_{(1,99)} = 168.75$, $p < .001$) on the perception of *controllability*, being due to higher objective controllability of the aversive situations than for the loss situations.

Both types of situation also reveal a strong decrement in controllability over the course of the episodes ($F_{(1,99)} = 150.41$, $p < .001$). There is no interaction effect between type of stressor (situation) and process, this means that there is no mutual influence between the two types of stressor and the course of the episode.

For subjects' perception of *changeability* there are similar effects regarding type of stressor ($F_{(1,99)} = 67.42$, $p < .001$) and over the course of the episode ($F_{(1,99)} = 67.75$, $p < .001$). The probability that the situation will change by its own dynamics is perceived as significantly lower in the loss and failure situations than in the aversive ones. If the stressor remains unchanged in the course of the episode, the expectation for a change is lowered. There is no interaction effect.

The impact of the situation and the process on the (perceived) possibility of a positive outcome, given either optimum response or the situation's own dynamics (controllability and changeability taken together), demonstrated a strongly lowered gross expectation for a positive outcome.

The *negative valence* was not perceived differently over the two classes of situations ($F_{(1,99)} = 2.31$; n.s.), nor is there a difference between the beginning of the episode and its continuation ($F_{(1,99)} = 2.08$; n.s.). But where the (hypothetical) end of the episodes described in phase 3 is concerned, there is a very strong effect of a positive vs. negative outcome, which is as predicted ($F_{(1,99)} = 701.92$; $p < .001$).

Interaction effects which occur between situation and process are due to situation-specific factors in the course of an episode. In the aversive episodes, the negative valence increases (from mean = 2.57 to mean = 2.73 including a significant single repeated effect), but it does not do so in loss and failure episodes. A similar result is produced regarding the influence of different outcomes. There is an interaction effect between outcome and situation, which indicates that the contrast of valence between positive and negative outcome is perceived as being stronger for loss and failure than for aversive episodes. The (hypothetical) end of the aversive episodes, which are shorter lasting, may produce more rapid decreases of arousal than it would for the lost/failure situations, which have more long-term implications regarding consequences. That may refer to the distinction of cognitive versus somatic anxiety, e.g. loss/failure involve more rumination than a clear termination of an aversive event.

Table 5. The impact of situation and process on appraisals, emotions, and goals (SCPQ final version; N=100)

		situations loss/ failure		aversive/ ambiguous		effects situation	process	situation x process
		M	s	M	s	F	F	F
appraisals of the situations:								
controllability	beginning	2.57	0.68	3.15	0.57	168.75[d]	150.41[d]	1.40
	continuation	2.08	0.71	2.73	0.64			
changeability	beginning	1.41	0.48	1.76	0.59	67.42[d]	67.75[d]	0.64
	continuation	1.12	0.56	1.51	0.62			
negative valence	beginning	2.75	0.53	2.57	0.62	2.31	2.08	31.12[d]
	continuation	2.67	0.54	2.73	0.66			
	outcome neg	2.99	0.69	2.79	0.69	0.10	701.92[d]	25.95[d]
	outcome pos	0.90	0.56	1.08	0.64			
emotional reactions*:								
anxious/nervous	beginning	1.96	0.56	1.97	0.63	0.58	611.37[d]	4.59[c]
	continuation	2.05	0.60	1.97	0.72			
	outcome neg	1.86	0.62	1.94	0.77			
	outcome pos	3.91	0.65	3.78	0.61			
depressed/sad	beginning	1.87	0.55	2.11	0.57	10.28[c]	521.55[d]	30.06[d]
	continuation	1.84	0.61	1.99	0.61			
	outcome neg	1.57	0.72	1.86	0.75			
	outcome pos	3.75	0.73	3.54	0.68			
aggressive/angry	beginning	2.28	0.59	2.19	0.66	13.66[d]	440.48[d]	6.92[d]
	continuation	2.21	0.63	1.95	0.74			
	outcome neg	2.00	0.77	2.00	0.79			
	outcome pos	3.87	0.73	3.65	0.67			
coping goals and intentions:								
alloplastic	beginning	2.25	0.32	2.17	0.35	19.28[d]	200.55[d]	185.80[d]
change	continuation	1.72	0.34	2.12	0.42			
emotional equi-	beginning	1.96	0.59	2.13	0.49	10.92[c]	6.26[b]	28.77[d]
librium	continuation	2.07	0.57	2.09	0.53			
self-esteem equi-	beginning	1.95	0.59	2.21	0.51	28.28[d]	14.44[d]	32.18[d]
librium	continuation	2.08	0.56	2.21	0.51			

[a] $p<.10$; [b] $p<.05$; [c] $p<.01$; [d] $p<.001$; * high values indicate low intensities of emotions

Taken together, the subjective appraisals of the situations and their change over time fit hypothesis (1) well, reflecting the objective built-in characteristics of the model conditions. The results for perceived controllability and changeability show strong situation effects as well as having being influenced by the course of the episode. This is a necessary precondition for subsequent differences in stress emotions, coping intentions and coping efforts as would be predicted by our situation-behavior model.

Emotional reactions (see table 5)

As table 5 shows, different stressful emotions are reported in the two different types of situations. If all 3 phases of the episodes are taken together it can be seen that there are more depressed and less aggressive feelings in the loss/failure episodes and vice versa in the aversive episodes ($F_{(1,99)} = 10.28$; $p < .001$ for depressed emotions; $F_{(1,99)} = 13.66$; $p < .001$ for aggressive feelings). For feeling anxious/nervous, there is no overall situation effect. There are also strong effects for all three emotional dimensions due to the negative/positive outcome in phase 3. The interaction effects ($F_{(3,97)} = 4.59$; $p < .01$ for anxiety; $F_{(3,97)} = 30.06$; $p < .001$ for feeling depressed; and $F_{(3,97)} = 6.92$; $p < .001$ for feeling aggressive) between situation and time demonstrate stressor-specific courses of stress emotions.

Coping goals and intentions (see table 5)

Table 5 shows also significant changes in the *alloplastic goal* of active influence on stressor (or preventing a probable loss) due to situation ($F_{(1,99)} = 19.28$, $p < .001$), time ($F_{(1,99)} = 200.55$; $p < .001$) and their interaction ($F_{(1,99)} = 185.80$; $p < .001$). In the situations of loss, with less gross and net controllability, subjects show a lower level of alloplastic intention (and more switch to the substitution goal) than in the aversive situations. There the intention of having assertive influence on the stressor changes only slightly. These results confirm hypothesis (4.1).

The *autoplastic goals* to preserve emotional status and self-esteem (equilibration) are also significantly affected by situation, time, and their interaction. The social *aversive situations* seem to augment the subjects' intentions for system-internal adaptation, because both the above intentions are stronger $(F_{(1,99)} = 10.92; \ p < .001; \ F_{(1,99)} = 29.28; \ p < .001)$. The *course* of the episodes has a similar influence, as time obviously affects the wish to stay calm or to preserve self-esteem $(F_{(1,99)} = 6.24; \ p < .05; \ F_{(1,99)} = 14.44; \ p < .001)$. The interaction effects indicate an augmentation of both system-internal intentions in the loss or failure episodes, whereas they remain on the same level in the aversive situations.

Environment-directed coping behavior (see table 6)

The results indicate clearly an effect of type of stressor and of time - the course of the episode - on the efforts made to influence the situation. The probability for *active influence* on the aversive stressor is much higher than for active intervention against loss or failure, as shown at the beginning (mean = 2.93 vs. 2.46) and in the continuation (mean = 2.72 vs. 2.16) of the episodes $(F_{(1,99)} = 82.99; \ p < .001)$. In both classes of situation the continuation of the stressful event from phase 1 to phase 2 produces a highly significant reduction in activity (mean = 2.64 to 2.16 and mean = 2.93 to 2.72; $F_{(1,99)} = 60.03; \ p < .001)$. In aversive situations, the probability for active influence is reduced less than it is in loss/failure episodes, indicated by an interaction tendency between situation and time $(F_{(1,99)} = 3.41; \ p < .10)$. This interaction trend is due to the persistence of situation-directed influence, given a higher level of controllability. The results are consistent with hypothesis (2).

The prediction concerning *passivity*, i.e. that subjects would be more hesitant and resigned in less controllable situation (hypothesis 2.2) is not confirmed $(F_{(1,99)} = 0.15; \ n.s.)$. There is, however, a significant time effect $(F_{(1,99)} = 11.37; \ p < .001)$ which shows that passivity increases from the beginning through to the continuation of both types of episodes. This corresponds with the reduction of perceived controllability from phase 1 to phase 2. There is no interaction effect between stressor type and time.

Self-directed coping behavior (see table 6)

The self-directed coping efforts measured by the questionnaire include different intrapsychic - and, to some extent, instrumental - behaviors, the function of which are to change the representation of the situation (or its components), to change the evaluations and goals, or to palliate emotions (the latter being a behavior directed to emotion as a situation element as it is given within the person, e.g. arousal). In addition inner intra- vs. extrapunitive responses are looked at.

As predicted in hypothesis (3), there are situation effects on *representation-oriented* behavior. In the more controllable aversive episodes, the probability of searching for (further) information is slightly higher ($F_{(1,99)}=3.04$; $p<.10$), whereas information suppression is somewhat lower ($F_{(1,99)}=3.26$; $p<.10$) than in the loss/failure episodes. From the beginning of the stressful event to its continuation (as described in the SCPQ episodes), the subjects obviously try to modify their representation of the stressor (process effects): they are less likely to search for information ($F_{(1,99)}=4.85$; $p<.05$) and more likely to suppress information ($F_{(1,99)}=39.20$; $p<.001$).

Table 6. The impact of situation and process on coping (SCPQ final version; N=100)

		situations loss/ failure		aversive/ ambiguous		effects situation	process	situation x process
		M	s	M	s	F	F	F
environment-directed coping:								
active influence	beginning	2.46	0.62	2.93	0.53	82.99[d]	60.03[d]	3.41[a]
	continuation	2.16	0.66	2.72	0.59			
passivity	beginning	1.40	0.51	1.42	0.52	0.15	11.37[c]	0.00
	continuation	1.49	0.51	1.50	0.53			
self-directed coping:								
search for	beginning	3.13	0.51	3.17	0.51	3.04[a]	4.85[b]	0.50
information	continuation	3.07	0.50	3.14	0.51			
suppression of	beginning	1.05	0.52	1.03	0.49	3.26[a]	39.20[d]	5.86[b]
information	continuation	1.26	0.57	1.14	0.53			
re-evaluation	beginning	2.14	0.57	2.24	0.59	0.69	0.87	9.82[c]
	continuation	2.23	0.55	2.19	0.64			
palliation	beginning	1.85	0.75	1.90	0.70	0.12	7.01[c]	2.87[a]
	continuation	1.95	0.76	1.93	0.77			
self-blaming	beginning	1.50	0.41	1.71	0.51	9.47[c]	2.92[a]	26.27[d]
	continuation	1.57	0.53	1.57	0.54			
other-blaming	beginning	1.88	0.51	1.99	0.60	17.96[d]	160.28[d]	7.99[c]
	continuation	2.10	0.53	2.32	0.64			

[a] $p<.10$; [b] $p<.05$; [c] $p<.01$; [d] $p<.001$;

For *evaluation-oriented* coping efforts, there is an interaction effect of situation-by-time ($F_{(1,99)}=9.82$; $p<.001$), which shows an inverted, situation-specific tendency to re-evaluate the relevance or valence of the actual stressor. This is in accord with hypothesis (4.2). In the course of loss/failure episodes the tendency to re-evaluate (or reappraise) is slightly increased whereas it is reduced in the course of aversive episodes.

Figure 6. Processes of appraisal, coping goal and behavior in different situations (aversive vs. loss/failure; beginning = T1, continuation = T2; SCPQ final version; N = 100)

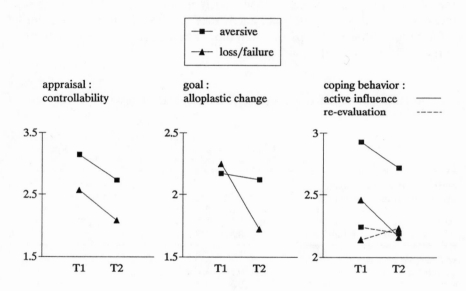

Palliation is increased from phase 1 to phase 2 ($F_{(1,99)} = 7.01$; $p < .001$), but there is no situation effect.

Type of stressor strongly modifies *self-blaming* ($F_{(1,99)} = 9.47$; $p < .001$) and *other-blaming* responses ($F_{(1,99)} = 17.96$; $p < .001$) whereas aversive episodes produce more blaming, punitive activities. This is an important finding. Additionally there is a very significant time effect ($F_{(1,99)} = 160.28$; $p < .001$) which strengthens other-blaming cognitions in the course of the episodes, when the stressor's intensity remains unchanged. The two significant interaction effects demonstrate situation-specific process effects.

Figure 6 depicts the main results concerning the hypotheses.

Discussion

The intention in this chapter was to demonstrate the influence of situation and process factors on stress and coping behavior, according to the predictions of the situation-behavior model. A different situation may arise due to type of stressor or over time, depending on the course of a stressful event. A harmless situation may turn into a really stressful one, when there is less control and more relevance (valence) of the looming event. There are substantial differences shown in certain coping tendencies, emotional pattern, and intentions. Also, so-called dysfunctional coping seems in many cases to be adaptive as regards other stressors and/or when the situation changes.

The subjects reported their appraisals, emotions, coping intentions and coping efforts in the face of standard stimulus episodes of the SCPQ which described the course of a stressful life event in three steps. The results reflect probable reactions in hypothetical situations, given the person's willingness and ability to describe (self-report). But the results clearly show effects of type of stressor (short-term social aversive vs. long-term loss and failure events), of process, i.e. the course of the stressful episode, and their interaction. The latter doesn't correspond to the 'statistical interaction' term used in the interactionist debate. The interaction which was analysed and statistically tested here, rather reflects different changes over time (from phase 1 to phase 2) which are (associated with or) specific to different prototypical stressors (aversive vs. loss and failure, each one containing a defined set of characteristics).

Most of the results are consistent with the predictions. For 5 out of the 8 *coping* variables analysed here, the results were significant and according to the predictions. But the effects the type of stressor (situation) exerted differed by way of the various coping behaviors: The strongest effects (in terms of F ratio) were observed for the active influence of the subject on the stressor, and for blaming others and self. For re-evaluation and palliation there were no situation effects, but there was an influence due to the interaction of situation and time. The course of the episodes (time) influenced all coping variables apart from the re-evaluation-variable. In addition only passivity and search for information revealed no interaction effects. All in all, the results seem very clear and consistent.

External validity of the results is somewhat restricted by the representativeness of the situation set including their situation features and by the fact that the subjects described responses to hypothetical rather than real events. However, internal validity was satisfactory and theoretically coherent.

While it may be of value to analyse the global effects of situations vs. times in a more generalized study, it does actually seem to be fruitful to have a model - and a method - to analyze tendencies which reflect 'narrow traits', and which can be evaluated in their adaptational function.

4. A computer-assisted self-observation system

Meinrad Perrez & Michael Reicherts

Methods for recording stress and coping data

Recording of psychological aspects of coping with stress has, to date, been based mainly on self-report data. The various procedures implemented varied from completely standardized questionnaires with hypothetical situations - as described in chapter 2 - to narrative or well structured protocols in which the subjects described their experiences during stress episodes (e.g. diary methods; e.g. Weber & Laux, 1987; Fisher & Elder, 1990). In some questionnaires (S-R questionnaires) hypothetical situations are presented, subjects having to describe how they would react. This type of questionnaire allows the inclusion of objective parameters of situations or stressors demanding adaptation. Some questionnaires such as that of Folkman and Lazarus (1988) assess reactions to real life stressors. They permit the process of intrapersonal adaptation to be studied and refer to the person's perception of the stressors.

Previous questionnaires for recording modes of coping with stress traded their high economy for an uncertain validity. Pawlik and Buse (1982) remarked that the available methodological tools for registering behavior in the field (i.e. temporally and physically close to the behavior in question and without retrospective judgment of behavior) were indeed very poor. 'One would like to go as far as to say that Karl Bühler's historic description of psychology as a 'science of the soul without a soul' (Bühler, 1931) has been replaced by the present-day judgment of psychology as being a 'behavioral science without behavior'.'

The major advantage of questionnaires arises from the short time required for application. Yet they suffer from problems of inadequate representation and reporting of one's own behavior and experience (cf. Ericson & Simon, 1980). They would seem to depict self-concepts of coping behavior rather than real experience and behavior, especially if the time lag between the stress encounters and their description in a questionnaire or interview is great. For some psychopathological groups this effect may be particularly strong.

In addition to using the self-report procedures, one can study coping behavior via observation of physiological characteristics. Such observations have been commonly used in experiments (e.g., Fenz & Epstein, 1962), but, to date, rarely for diagnostic purposes. The latter is also true of the systematic observation of the psychological characteristics of the coping process. Horowitz and Wilner (1976) studied real stressors under experimental conditions, Zeitlin (1980) observed coping behavior in real situations and Hänggi and Schedle (1987) made observations using hypothetical situations.

Table 7. Matrix of situations and data sources for the recording of stress and coping behavior (examples)

Situations *Data sources*	hypothetical situations	laboratory situations with real or filmed stressors	real life situations in the field
self-description	Krohne, Wigand & Kiehl, 1985 Becker, 1984 Reicherts & Perrez, 1991 (SCPQ; UBV)	Krohne, 1986 Lazarus et al., 1963	Folkman & Lazarus, 1980 Folkman & Lazarus, 1988 (WC) Braukmann & Filipp, 1983 (SEBV; German version of the WC)
external observation of psychological characteristics		Horowitz & Becker, 1971 Horowitz & Wilner, 1976 Scherer et al., 1985	Mechanic, 1962 Zeitlin, 1980
external observation of physiological characteristics	Lang et al., 1983 Hänggi & Schedle, 1987	Lazarus et al., 1962 Otto, 1991 Scherer et al., 1985	Fenz & Epstein, 1962

The different methods used to record the psychological characteristics of coping behavior can be summarized in the following matrix, which differentiates between the data sources and the setting of the study or the way the situation is presented (table 7). For further discussion see also McGrath' (1982) classification of stress response indexes.

Computer-assisted self-observation: Goals and theoretical background

Pawlik and Buse (1982) developed a computer-assisted self-observation method that allowed reliable self-assessments of both environmental and psychological variables as well as field circumstances. This method inspired us to develop the COMRES method (*COM*puter-assisted *RE*cording *S*ystem). This makes possible the assessment of everyday stress and coping episodes. The most important goals in the development of a method for computer-assisted self-observation under field conditions were:

(1) The possibility of field recording of experiential and behavioral data, in order to reduce memory distortion due to the time lag between the occurrence of the stressful event and the assessment thereof. Also to facilitate the recording of information when the subject is still in the state of emotional arousal ('hot cognitions').
(2) The structured collection of psychologically relevant data.

The methods employed to achieve these goals were as follows:

(1) The minicomputer employed was about the size of a note pad (18 x 7 x 1.5 cm), could be carried around during everyday activities, and allowed the immediate entry of information after the stressful episode or even during the episode. Though the latter was not always possible, experience showed that in most cases it was possible. Thus, the time-span between the event and the assessment thereof was reduced, and cognitive distortions were kept at a minimum. The subjects recorded the 30 to 40 stressful episodes in the course of an average of 5 weeks.
(2) The self-assessment procedure was structured according to psychologically relevant features proposed in chapter 2, these also being used in the construction of the SCPQ questionnaire. It included dimensions measuring perception, emotion, goals, coping reactions, and causal attributions. According to Lazarus (1966), stress and coping episodes are

real events precipitated either externally or internally which tax or demand the psychological system of the individual, and which are interpreted and worked-out via this system. Such episodes have a temporal structure that begins with a disturbance of the homeostasis and is followed by attempts to re-establish psychological equilibrium.

The structure of the variables included in the self-observation procedure largely corresponds to the structure of the questionnaire, described in chapter 2. The difference lies in the absence of the hypothetical situation which in the questionnaire represents the standardized stimulus component.

Our method allows a free description of the stressful event and the structured, subjective assessment of the stressor, according to criteria of *valence, controllability, changeability, ambiguity, probability of reoccurrence* and *familiarity*. The subject's goal in the stressful situation can be freely described. Further, the subject's emotional status when faced with the stressor can be assessed. The method also differentiates between self-directed coping reactions (search for information, information repression, palliation, re-evaluation, inner other-blaming, and self-blaming) and environment-directed coping reactions (evasion, passivity, active influence, support through others). Further, data on coping efficiency (goal attainment, discrepancy between actual and ideal behavior), representativeness of one's own behavior, and causal attribution are gathered.

With this method it is also possible to observe long-term stress episodes - that is, the sequence of micro-episodes belonging to the same problem. In this way the sequence of micro-episodes resulting from a difficult decision can be observed and stored. In addition the overlap of several problems over a period of days or weeks can be studied in this manner. The COMRES system assumes that subjects have already been trained in self-observation. In other words, the users are not naive, but qualified self-observers.

The COMRES Method

The above-mentioned goals require (1) a simple, easy-to-use recording and rating system for the description and judgment of the most important characteristics of the respective stress situation and events, and (2) a system of categories for describing self- and environment-directed attempts at coping. In an initial experiment, the project workers themselves tried out various means. The pilot study resulted in several improvements of the initial variant.

Development of the computer program was oriented to criteria of software ergonomy (e.g., simple, user-friendly), safety of data entry and recording of data, economic memory organization, and work speed. Of major importance was the structuring of the user interface: once the program has been started, it presents the subject with a series of questions to be worked through using a series of answers. The basic pattern shown in figures 1, 2, and 3 in the appendix was employed to improve the quality of entry data.

Questions demanding a scaled answer were always displayed together with the numbered scale. The answer given was then shown on the computer display as the verbal label of the scale. This, in turn, was either corrected or confirmed. A 'help' key allowed the user to view the respective scale on the computer display at all times during the assessment. A particular problem was finding a structure flexible enough to allow users to break down and describe the episodes at their own discretion. For this purpose, we chose a program structure with which previously recorded descriptions could be reviewed and the new situation linked to the old one(s) by a special marking sequence. In this way episodes could be broken down in great detail, and overlapping or time-delayed processing and follow-up of multiple episodes could be performed. The program was written in BASIC.

The *general instruction* to use the self-assessment computer was 'Whenever You feel stressed, affected, excited or disturbed, try to record the situation directly on the computer!'. The stressor should also be recorded even if it is not yet over. We developed a *user manual* (Reicherts, Perrez & Matathia, 1986) to make the use of the computer easier and to improve the quality of the self-observation. It also allowed us to give the subjects an initial standardized training. In addition, the user manual had a stand-by function to help answer questions or solve problems which occurred and to give support to the subject.

This *event-sampling* method could be replaced or supplemented by a time-sampling procedure. Schwenkmezger and Schmitz-Friedhoff (1987) describe a time sampling self-observational method to record ongoing activities according to qualities such as valence, effort, and self-certainty.

Table 8. Variables of the COMRES self-observation system for stressful episodes

topic	type of input	rating levels	
characterization of the episode:			
episodic structure (initial vs. subseq. situation)	categorical	2	
short description	text	-	
appraisal of situation characteristics:			
controllability		6	(0;5)
changeability		6	(0;5)
negative valence	scales	6	(0;5)
ambiguity		6	(0;5)
probability of reoccurrence		6	(0;5)
familiarity		6	(0;5)
duration		5	(0;4)
emotional reactions:			
profile with 6 dimensions	scales	6	(0;5)
(anxious/nervous, depressed, aggressive,			
hesitant, lethargic, abandoned)			
additional description (optional)	text	-	
goal(s) of coping	text	-	
self-directed coping behavior:			
search for information		3	(0;2)
suppression of information		3	(0;2)
re-evaluation	scales	3	(0;2)
palliation		3	(0;2)
self-blaming		3	(0;2)
other-blaming		3	(0;2)
environment-directed coping behavior:			
active influence on stressor		3	(0;2)
evasion (escape, avoid)		3	(0;2)
passivity (hesitate, wait)	scales	3	(0;2)
help from others		3	(0;2)
additional description of active influence	text	-	
coping efficiency (to date):			
problem solving	scales	3	(0;2)
discrepancy ideal/real behavior		3	(0;2)
representativeness of behavior	scales	4	(0;3)
attribution of outcome:			
internal		4	(0;3)
external (persons)	scales	4	(0;3)
external (circumstances)		4	(0;3)
time and date	text	-	

Evaluation of the COMRES Method: First Results

The following questions have been studied with a sample of 60 subjects:

(1) reported situations: prototypes of stressful episodes
(2) reliability of the method,
(3) reactivity effects, and
(4) influence of 'social desirability' on the recording.

In the following sections we describe the findings related to the COM-RES method, assessing reliability, reactivity effects, social desirability, and practical applicability.

Sample and data collection

The sample consisted of 60 adults, 30 males and 30 females. The mean age was 26.0 years (std 4.4). The subjects were all university students; 80% of them were unmarried. About 22% of subjects lived alone, 27% with their partner or spouse, 5% with relatives, 43% shared an apartment with others, and 3% had other living arrangements.

About 73% of the sample reported having no somatic symptoms or diseases, 18% slight symptoms or diseases. The remaining 9% of subjects had either strong or very strong symptoms or diseases. On their psychological health status, about 27% reported experiencing no present problems, 52% had slight problems, and 21% had pronounced problems. Thus, all in all, we were dealing with a typical (advanced) student population in central Europe. The subjects were recruited from among students at the University of Fribourg and Bern (Switzerland); they received Sfr. 50.- for their participation.

The subjects were trained to use the system on the basis of the user's manual. They were also instructed to record at least 30 episodes.

Types of recorded situations

2381 episodes were recorded by the subjects, the mean number per subject was nearly 40 episodes during 4 to 5 weeks of self-observation. These episodes are very different. A few examples may illustrate the types of notes made by the subjects.

Example (1): 'My wife comes back home. I haven't prepared supper yet. She is angry.'

Example (2): 'I am startled by a German shepherd suddenly appearing as I am walking my dog.'

Example (3): 'I become upset because tomorrow I have an exam. May be I'm not well prepared and I feel shaky.'

The COMRES-method elicits different features of the experienced episodes as perceived by the subject; their controllability, changeability, valence, ambiguity, subjective probability of reoccurrence, the duration of the stressor, and the subject's familiarity with the situation. The question is whether this method can identify types of situations by an inductive multidimensional procedure.

Method for identifying types of situations

To answer the above question the total number of 2381 episodes stored was submitted to a cluster analysis. The formation of clusters was based on the weighted average distances method (Euclidean distances) with stepwise formation of centroids, and given maximum number of clusters (SPSSX method Quick Cluster), which was fixed according to the number of situation variables included (n=6; excluding 'probability of reoccurrence').

Results

The cluster analysis reveals three major types of situations which cover 66% of all episodes of the pool.

Type 1 situations: The greatest cluster (741 situations) is characterized by the following cluster means:
- fairly high controllability (3.2),
- low changeability (0.9),
- fairly high negative valence (3.4),
- high transparency (4.3), i.e. low ambiguity,
- relatively short duration (half an hour/one hour; 2.3),
- fairly high familiarity (3.4).
This type of situation concerns everyday matters - which are important

nonetheless - and which are perceived as fairly controllable. The stressor is relatively unambiguous and of short duration. Example (1) above, for instance, belongs to this cluster. It can be assumed that this kind of situation with high 'net' control (i.e. controllability exceeding by far changeability - 2.3 scale points) facilitates active coping and reduces the probability of re-evaluation.

Figure 7. Situation characteristics of three types of situations in stressful episodes

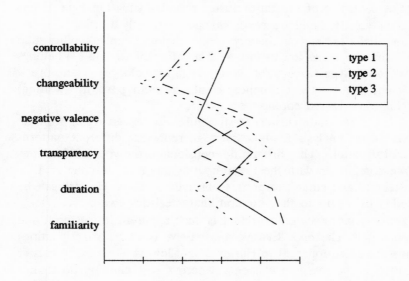

Type 2 situations: The second cluster holds 454 episodes. They are described by the following configuration of features (cluster means):
- fairly low controllability (2.2),
- low changeability (1.4)
- high negative valence (3.8),
- low transparency (2.3),
- longer duration (several hours, 4.3)
- and high familiarity (4.6).
The low 'net control' (0.8), and the low 'overall probability' of a positive outcome, combined with high valence and longer duration can be interpreted as the kind of stressful situation which tends to elicit depressive

and helpless feelings and passive and evasive coping responses. Example (2) belongs - except for its shorter duration - to this type.

Type 3 situations: The third cluster (382 episodes) is characterized as follows (cluster means):
- fairly high controllability (3.2)
- fairly changeability (2.8)
- fairly low negative valence (2.4)
- fairly high transparency (3.8),
- medium duration (2.9), and
- high familiarity (4.4).

The centroids of the third cluster reveal a situation type of low 'net control' (controllability exceeds changeability only a little: 0.3), and fairly low valence and ambiguity. Nevertheless, controllability and changeability are not as low as in type 2 situations. Example (3) belongs to this situation type (except for its low negative valence). Therefore it should elicit some active influence, combined with passivity (waiting) and evaluation-oriented coping responses.

These three main clusters of stressful episodes, emerging from an inductive cluster analysis method, seem to represent different patterns of stressful situations. They are multidimensional prototypes of situations which are compatible with the theoretical assumptions in chapter 1.
The emotional and coping responses observed in these clusters can be predicted with regard to the situation characteristics given:

Actively influencing on stressor is most apparent in cluster 1, and least apparent in cluster 2. Evasive and passive (waiting or resignation) behaviors are most apparent in cluster 2, and lowest apparent in cluster 1. Palliation is increased in cluster 2, whereas re-evaluation dominates in cluster 3. Stressful emotions of being depressed, nervous, and abandoned are increased in situation 2. Another type of prediction analysis referring to stressful situations is reported in more detail in chapter 5. It does not refer to an inductive (clustering) method but to an a priori typology proposing two types of situations which correspond with clusters 1 and 2 reported here.

Reliability

The calculation of the split-half reliability coefficients bases on the COMRES variables of the initial episodes only. This refers to events which had - according to the subject - no links to previously recorded stressful episodes. Initial episodes were numbered sequentially, divided odd-even, and the mean values for the two halves were calculated. The mean values of the even and odd episodes were then correlated, and the correlations were enhanced using the Spearman-Brown formula. Calculation of the split-half reliability values in this way was necessary because of the different actual events and their varying number recorded by the individual subjects (cf. Pawlik & Buse, 1982). This reliability test measures cross-situational stability, i.e. *consistency*, of the person's stress and coping behavior.

The mean reliability (after z transformation) for all COMRES variables was $r_{tt} = .85$ for the average 30.3 episodes. As expected, the consistency was somewhat smaller for the more context-dependent variables in environment-oriented coping (activity, passivity, evasion, social support) and for the attribution tendencies (own behavior, behavior of others, circumstances), the mean r_{tt} being .77 and .81 respectively (see for example McCrae, 1989). Here, the situation variance had a greater effect than in the case of emotions (mean $r_{tt} = .85$), situation appraisal (.87), self-directed coping behavior (.83) and subjective representativeness (.86). Yet, since we are dealing here with the self-observations and self-perceptions from very heterogeneous stress situations for each subject, the consistency may generally be considered to be satisfactory. The same is true for *stability* over time (see chapter 5, trait based prediction).

Reactivity

The possibility that self-observation of one's own reaction toward psychological stress over a period of several weeks can have an influence on the behavior in question cannot be ruled out. The subject may learn to perceive important aspects of his or her behavior in such situations in a better and more precise fashion, which may then influence the cognitive structure in the way suggested by Schroder, Driver, and Streufert (1967) and lead to modified information processing.

In order to test for reactivity, the recorded episodes were divided in half according to their temporal rank in the episode sequence. Thus episodes of the first protocol half were aggregated and compared with the aggregated episodes of the second part of the sequence. The variances of the first vs. second half than were analysed for each variable (see table 9, columns on the right side).

Table 7: COMRES reliability and reactivity over time (all r_{12} p<.001)

	M_1 odd	M_2 even	s_1	s_2	r_{12}	r_{tt}	M_{t1} half 1	M_{t2} half 2	s_{t1}	s_{t2}	time F
appraisal of situation characteristics:						(.87)					
controllability	2.71	2.85	.58	.60	.66	.80	2.82	2.73	.58	.58	0.82
changeability	1.56	1.50	.57	.61	.72	.84	1.51	1.55	.57	.62	0.76
negative valence	2.86	2.90	.61	.68	.82	.90	2.83	2.92	.62	.68	3.45[a]
ambiguity	3.59	3.65	.80	.75	.80	.89	3.62	3.62	.71	.82	0.02
probability of reoccurr.	2.76	2.77	.64	.68	.70	.82	2.87	2.66	.60	.74	6.44[b]
familiarity with situation	2.95	3.05	.61	.62	.82	.90	3.14	2.87	.65	.64	13.35[d]
duration	2.42	2.36	.59	.63	.85	.92	2.39	2.37	.61	.63	0.29
emotional reactions:*						(.85)					
anxious/nervous	2.03	2.04	.54	.56	.64	.78	1.96	2.11	.51	.59	5.84[b]
depressed	2.21	2.24	.54	.55	.79	.88	2.20	2.26	.55	.57	1.82
aggressive	2.53	2.53	.52	.56	.71	.83	2.47	2.58	.53	.56	2.69
hesitant	2.61	2.68	.49	.58	.69	.82	2.62	2.65	.58	.51	0.34
lethargic	2.66	2.72	.46	.54	.61	.76	2.70	2.68	.49	.52	0.13
abandoned	2.10	2.14	.65	.67	.85	.92	2.08	2.17	.62	.74	1.11
self-directed coping behavior:						(.87)					
search for information	1.12	1.15	.45	.43	.88	.94	1.18	1.09	.46	.44	4.33[b]
suppression of informat.	0.69	0.64	.31	.30	.66	.80	0.63	0.69	.30	.33	2.25
re-evaluation	0.69	0.72	.41	.43	.78	.88	0.73	0.68	.46	.40	0.89
palliation	0.89	0.90	.39	.40	.85	.92	0.85	0.94	.42	.43	2.57
self-blaming	0.73	0.73	.33	.36	.67	.80	0.71	0.74	.36	.36	0.12
other-blaming	0.81	0.83	.37	.40	.71	.83	0.82	0.81	.37	.40	0.34
environment-directed coping behavior:						(.77)					
active influence on stress	1.03	1.13	.32	.34	.60	.75	1.12	1.04	.34	.33	2.50
evasion (escape, avoid)	0.62	0.61	.31	.31	.56	.72	0.57	0.65	.27	.33	9.17[c]
passivity (wait, resign)	0.93	0.87	.31	.29	.55	.71	0.86	0.94	.34	.28	3.20[a]
help from others	0.49	0.51	.30	.31	.76	.87	0.51	0.49	.31	.33	0.70
coping efficiency:						(.87)					
problem solving	0.97	1.04	.39	.34	.72	.84	0.97	1.03	.36	.37	1.84
discrep. ideal/real behav.	1.15	1.13	.45	.44	.81	.90	1.15	1.11	.42	.49	1.70
representativ. of behavior:	1.96	1.99	.32	.35	.63	.77	1.98	1.97	.34	.35	0.01
attribution of outcome:						(.81)					
internal	1.59	1.64	.40	.40	.63	.77	1.59	1.63	.38	.46	0.56
external (persons)	1.01	0.97	.37	.41	.69	.81	1.03	0.96	.39	.40	2.74
external (circumstances)	1.07	1.04	.42	.43	.73	.85	1.09	1.03	.42	.45	2.07
total						(.85)					

[a] p<.10; [b] p<.05; [c] p<.01; [d] p<.001; * high values indicate low intensities of emotions

The results point to relatively few changes overall over the course of the period of self-observation. For coping attempts there was an increase in the tendency toward evasion as well as passivity. Yet there was, strikingly enough, also a decrease in the (inner) search for information. With emotional stress reactions there was a tendency towards lower values only for feeling anxious/nervous. The fact that the situations occurring in the second half of the assessment period were judged as being less familiar and as having a lower probability of recurring suggests that subjectively more unusual events were being experienced in the second half of the assessment period, and were faced with somewhat modified coping reactions. Whether the stress was truly different (for example, when some of the students taking their exams actually enter the examination phase) or whether the effect over the course of the assessment period in fact reflects the reactivity of the self-observation (an increasing 'openness' toward unusual stress and the 'confession' of dysfunctional coping methods), cannot be decided with certainty. The low level of reactivity generally, as well as the relatively high reliability found, seems to show that the COMRES system provides useful data for the diagnosis of coping with stress. A difference in reactivity effects dependent on different modes of defense (repression, sensitization; cf. Krohne, 1986) were in any case hardly perceptible (Reicherts & Perrez, 1990).

Social desirability

For the validity of the method it is important to know the extent to which tendencies of social desirability are present in the self-observation and the recording thereof. This is important even when there are no other data sources available (e.g., observation through others) for the event in question. The extent to which the different aspects of the self-described stress process are associated with social desirability are examined. Crowne and Marlowe's (1960) concept and SDS Scale measure (German version of Lück and Timaeus, 1969) were used to this end.

The correlations of the mean values of the self-observation variables showed the following relationships with social desirability. The higher the social desirability, the greater the tendency to perceive situations as less changeable ($r=-.22$; $p<.10$) and the lower the tendency towards feelings of aggressivity ($r=-.30$; $p<.05$) and other-blaming ($r=-.22$; $p<.10$). The correlations to all other COMRES variables are not significant. Thus, there are indeed some plausible relationships between individual aspects of this self-observation method and social desirability. However, their influence overall doesn't seem strong enough to seriously reduce the validity of the diagnostic information gathered using the COMRES method. And when COMRES is used as an instrument for preparing someone for therapy and for accompanying diagnostic measures, clearly one should find that the effects of social desirability are even smaller.

Practical application of COMRES

Our first experience has shown that COMRES is a practical and useful method for the event-oriented self-observation of stress and coping. It is easy to carry and data was often directly recorded. The average time necessary for an entry was about 5 minutes. In the post-interview, 80% of the subjects reported a tendency towards increased self-reflection during the experiment, and 50% noted small changes in their own behavior and experience during the assessment. This - in addition to other insights gained during the post-interview - indicates the generally positive acceptance of the method. Yet some of the subjects did not view the assessment completely positively. Whereas in the individual assessments they judged their own coping behavior and experience for the most part as being 'typical', they later reduced their judgment of the representativeness of the described events by half. This is apparently due to the fact that individual, subjectively important events also took place which some subjects did not 'reveal' to their computer. Thus, in the light of these reserved events, some subjects' event samples were incomplete. This restriction does not, however, necessarily affect the validity of the results with respect to correlations between stressful situations and reactions to them, since it does not have a bearing on the representativeness of reactions in the presence of events. Rather it concerns the representativeness of the events themselves.

Problems arising during data collection seem to be correlated with the motivation of the individual subject(s). This view is confirmed from initial use of the method in clinical contexts with alcoholics and women suffering from bulimia; the degree of suffering and therapeutic motivation increases the conscientiousness with which recording with COMRES is done (see also the case study in chapter 11). Again, the face validity of the self-observation categories employed seems to further the acceptance of the method among users. Difficulties in the use of computer techniques decline even among non-students after proper training of the subjects is completed.

Summary and outlook

In summary, the main characteristics of the COMRES method give some hope for its usefulness regarding most of the self-observation variables. The situation prototypes emerging from event sampling are plausible, reliability is satisfactory, reactivity effects over time are minimal and the effects of social desirability are limited. Self-observation in everyday stress situations over a period of several weeks and the subsequent summation of subjective mean values is thus not only methodologically possible, it is indeed quite effective. The approach (trained self-observation of everyday stress) and the method used (multi-dimensional assessment with pocket computer) resulted in satisfactory findings, at least for the student population studied.

In addition to measuring stress and coping, the method opens up new approaches to the study of the psychology of everyday life. Many of the methodological problems related to questionnaires and interviews are not associated with this new access to subjective data: the time lag between stressful event and its recording can be minimized; the chaining of episodes over time can be easily represented (which is more complicated if it is done by usual diary method); the computer-aided self-observation system can adapt the selection of questions to specific features of situations or peculiarities of the scientific problem. The interviewer/ee bias is eliminated.

Initial analysis of the relationships between characteristics of coping with stress and various indicators of mental health reveal, on the group level, relevant correlations with a number of indicators as well as with Beck's Depression Inventory and the State-Trait-Anxiety Inventory (see chapter 9).

On the individual level the relationships between situation characteristics as perceived by the subject and the subject's attempts at coping was particularly interesting. Such rules (strategies) and regularities in coping behavior can be studied using the contingency-based method of behavior rule conformity analysis (see chapter 11; also including a case study). This could lead to personal stress and coping scores including criterion-oriented measurement in the field, possibly even leading to situation-specific recommendations about how to cope with stress.

The development of this method carries with it the hope that it may be possible to expand even further this new methodology of self-observation in the field. Thus, it could become useful for theory-guided recording and direct analysis of stress and coping behavior. In addition, by simplifying the structure of the questions and the overall operation of the system, by improving the safety of use, and by implementing analysis programs directly into the COMRES computer, it is possible to develop the idea of a *'external memory against stress'* especially if the method is employed in a clinical and health care surrounding.

5. Prediction of stress and coping behavior in the natural setting

Michael Reicherts & Meinrad Perrez

Introduction

The concept of behavior being predictable presupposes that behavior follows laws and rules. Mainstream research on trait-based approaches during the last decades concentrated on questions concerning longitudinal consistency (i.e. stability) and cross-situational consistency. Magnusson & Endler (1977) differentiated the latter by distinguishing different parameters for reactions, focusing on reactions to similar vs. dissimilar situations. A statistical paradigm, factor analysis, largely guided the whole approach along with the later utilisation of a model based on analysis of variance, after the concept of situation-person-interaction had been introduced. This approach was mainly based on questionnaire data.

Hempel (1965) analysed the logical structure of prediction in terms of the syllogism of causal explanation. For causal explanation and causally founded prediction, knowledge of the lawfulness of behavior is a conditio sine qua non. Causally founded predictions are distinguished from rational predictions (Stegmüller, 1983). For the latter only empirically confirmed correlations between antecedent indicators or symptoms and the predicted behavior are needed. Hence, the values of a theory-less questionnaire may predict some later behavior probabilities of a person or a group. We call this kind of prediction 'blind' prediction. Some of the approaches which seek to predict behavior according to general dispositions (traits) and by situation-person interaction belong to this prediction family. On the other hand, causally founded predictions are deduced or induced from *confirmed laws* of behavior and *singular antecedent conditions*, i.e. specific relevant circumstances that are antecedent to the event to predict. They are relevant singular conditions if they are causally linked with the event to be predicted.

We try to analyse the predictability of certain types of behavior

(a) in the context of certain hypotheses concerning the influence of situation parameters on behavior as perceived by the subject, and (b) on the basis of computer-aided self-observational field data.

The *underlying theory postulates* - as described in chapter 1 - that the perception of objective controllability, changeability and valence of the stressful situation is a relevant antecedent condition for coping behavior. Controllability is defined as the probability that a situation can be influenced by the person's best available reaction. Changeability is defined as the probability that a situation will change according to its own dynamic. The following lawful hypotheses give the 'nucleus' of the theory, namely:

(1) the higher the perceived controllability of a situation in relation to its changeability (the 'net' control) and the higher the valence, then the higher the probability for active influence on situation as coping behavior;

(2) the more controllability is equal to changeability, and the more the overall chance of positive outcome for the situation approximates 50/50, then the stronger will be the tendency to remain passive (hesitation or resignation);

(3) the lower the overall chance of a positive outcome (the 'gross' control), the stronger the tendency to escape or avoid. In addition the more negative the valence of the situation, given a low or middle controllability value, then the higher the probability for evasive coping behavior.

Predictability of behavior with respect to these theoretical assumptions were analysed and the results obtained compared with predictions without theoretical assumptions. (Further predictions concerning emotional reactions and self-directed intrapsychic coping efforts are presented in part 3.)

Method

Features of *stressor-perception/appraisal* and *coping behavior* were assessed by the COMRES self-observation method (see chapter 4).

Subjects

The sample consists of the 60 undergraduate students - described in chapter 4 - from the universities of Fribourg and Bern (Switzerland). They were recruited by other students, and received sF 50.- for participation. There was an equal number of male and female participants. The mean age was 26 years (std=4.4).

Procedure

The event sequence of each subject was split according to the first and the second half of the sequence, so that 2 subsamples were obtained for each time period. The mean behavior ratings stemming from these time period subsamples were used as aggregated behavior indicators. The episodes of each half are split using a theory-based three-dimensional classification criterion involving two classes of situations (table 10).

Table 10. Classification of stressful situations for predictions in the natural setting

perceived situation characteristics	classification criteria for situation classes			
	class 1		class 2	
controllability	low-middle	gross & net control not high	high	gross & net control high
changeability	low-middle		high	
negative valence	high		low-middle	

This procedure permitted two subsamples to be obtained for each person, split by time (sequence). Each subsample contained two situation classes, according to a 2x2 factors repeated measurement design (2 situations x 2 times). A minimum criterion of 3 episodes per situation class and time period (of each subject) was set. The aggregated measures are therefore based on at least 3 separate occasions. This procedure excluded some subjects, leaving a sample of 50 subjects.

Reliability and validity of the method

Estimations of reliability, reactivity, and social desirability of the self-observation method are described in chapter 4. Due to the two-dimensional, four-fold concept of repression-sensitization as proposed by Krohne (1986) and others there are differences only in feelings of depression and abandonment: 'sensitizer' and 'high anxious' people reporting more of them (see Reicherts & Perrez, 1990).

In order to analyse *external validity* of the method, the S-R-S-R process questionnaire SCPQ (see chapter 2) was used, which asks for the same responses as the self-observational system does (i.e. ratings of situation appraisals, emotional, and coping behaviors etc.). There was high predictive correlation between questionnaire and self-report data for global tendencies of emotional reaction variables (mean $r = .64$) and self-directed coping efforts (mean $r = .58$). Situation appraisals (mean $r = .37$) and environment-directed coping efforts (mean $r = .24$) were less well correlated with the corresponding response type in the process questionnaire.

Results

As outlined above, a distinction should be made between different types of psychological prediction of behavior according to the following:

(1.1) The global, situation-unspecific prediction of behavior grounded on generalized dispositions ('big' traits) of the subjects,

(1.2) the situation-specific prediction on the basis of more or less situation specific dispositions ('narrow' traits),

(2) the situation-specific prediction on the basis of a psychological theory (by explanative interpretation; e.g. Bunge, 1967), which connects the behavior to be predicted with certain characteristics of the perceived situation 'within' the person concerned.

Trait-based prediction

The global, situation-unspecific behavior strength as observed and described by the subject can be predicted as follows; behavioral tendencies associated with each stress and coping variables are aggregated for the first and the second half of the subjects' assessment series. Behavior tendencies in the later period are then predicted by a 'law-like' hypothesis (H: there is stability of behavior B_i over certain time) and a single condition (P has the tendency to behave B_i in period T_i). Conclusion: P has the tendency to behave B_i in the following period T_{i+1}.

A similar rationale is applied to predict behavior in different situations S_j; it refers to the hypothesis of transsituational consistency. For such predictions the correlation/regression model is usually used. The mean behavior strength stemming from several episodes (relating the subjects' earlier position within the distribution of the values in a sample of other subjects to its later position) serves as predictor for a criterion given by another, later mean behavior value.

In our study the relationship between these global over-time correlations of stress and coping variables and general dispositions or traits is shown in table 11 (1st column).

Table 11. Correlations between periods 1 and 2 over all situations, and class 1 and 2

	situations		
	all	class 2	class 1
mean number of episodes n	41.8	25.1	16.7
emotional reactions: (mean)	.70	.71	.31
anxious/nervous	.71	.79	-.07
depressed	.70	.77	.26
aggressive	.64	.75	.07
hesitant	.70	.58	.61
lethargic	.70	.56	.46
abandoned	.77	.77	.44
environment-directed coping: (mean)	.61	.62	.46
evasion/avoidance	.74	.76	.46
passivity/hesitation	.52	.54	.43
active influence	.57	.55	.48
using social support	.60	.58	.46
self-directed coping behavior: (mean)	.63	.68	.59
palliation	.57	.70	.72
re-evaluation	.68	.61	.65
self-blaming	.64	.71	.61
other-blaming	.62	.70	.31
total	.66	.68	.44

note: coefficients corrected according to Spearman-Brown formula; all correlation means based on z-transformed coefficients

The *environment-directed* coping behaviors are correlated with a mean of $r = .61$ (all correlations highly significant). This correlation means that you can predict 37% the variance from phase 1 to phase 2). There is a higher correlation for evasion/avoidance as coping behavior type ($r=.74$) than passivity ($r=.52$); 'using social support' ($r=.60$) and 'active influence on stressor' ($r=.57$) fall between these correlations.

The *self-directed* coping behaviors in period 1 and period 2 are similarly related, their mean being $r=.63$. Behavior strength in period 1 predicts about 40% of the variance in period 2. Re-evaluation as self-directed coping behavior is more stable ($r=.68$) than palliation ($r=.57$) and blaming self ($r=.64$) or others ($r=.62$).

On the other hand the *emotional reaction* or feeling variables are more stable from period 1 to period 2. The strongest correlation reaches $r=.77$ for feeling 'abandoned' whereas feeling 'aggressive' seems less stable ($r=.64$). All the other correlations are about $r=.70$. For emotional reactions the mean is $r=.71$, which indicates a somewhat higher stability than for the coping behavior variables.

Predictions using the situation-*specific* trait concept show similar results for situations of class 2 ('gross' and 'net' controllability relatively high; negative valence low to middle). Best predicted are emotional reactions (mean $r=.71$), and self-directed coping tendencies are somewhat better predicted ($r=.68$) than using the global *un*specific trait. Environment-directed predictions are as good for specific as for unspecific traits. In situation class 1 (controllability and changeability low to middle, negative valence high) emotions and coping behaviors are less well predicted (mean $r=.44$). Only for self-directed coping the correlation ($r=.59$) reaches the level of the situation class 2. Taken together, these results reveal no improvement when predictions are based on situation-specific traits.

Michael (1966; see also Rosenthal & Rubin, 1982) proposed a concept to evaluate the predictive validity of product-moment correlation coefficients. Michael's formula allows estimation of the probability of 'hits' in predicting the subject's later position relative to the sample median by means of his earlier position over or under the median. According to this, a mean correlation between time 1 and time 2 of $r=.61$ of the environment-directed coping variables allows us to predict the right position over/under the sample median for about 71% of the subjects. For the correlations of the emotional variables (mean $r=.71$) the predicted proportion of people over resp. under the sample median is about 76%. Both values, 72% and 76%, are substantially better then prediction by chance, which is correct for 50% of the cases. It should be emphasized that this kind of prediction deals with the position of the subject with respect to the subjects' behavior relative to a group or a sample, no matter if it be high or low.

Theory-based prediction

Prediction using a situation-behavior theory of stress and coping is based on the assumption that the subject takes into account some situation characteristics (like controllability, or valence) to select and govern his behavior. This, in turn, serves to realize the subject's goals. Prediction by the situation-behavior-theory of stress and coping is based on the lawful assumption mentioned earlier, namely that the subject's perception of controllability, changeability and valence of the stressful situation permits the prediction of certain types of coping behavior.

    According to the above theory a stronger evasion/avoidance tendency would be expected in situation 1 than in situation 2, and more hesitation/resignation and use of social support, and less active influence on the situation would also be expected. Secondly, more palliation of negative affect would be expected in low controllable and highly aversive situations like type 1, along with more blaming activity - blaming oneself as well as others - and less re-evaluation activity (because the strong negative valence makes it more difficult to change evaluations and/or standards immediately). Thirdly, more fearful, depressed, and aggressive emotional reactions would be expected as well as feeling more hesitant, lethargic and abandoned in situations of low control and high negative valence.

    The measure used here is a prediction ratio (pr): the number of subjects whose behavior is correctly predicted divided by the total of predictions made. The prediction is based on the ordinal comparison of the subjects' summed up behavior ratings in situation class 1 vs. class 2. The results are shown in table 12 (1st column).

The predictions for *environment-directed* coping hold true for 65% of the cases (median of prediction ratio pr). Best predicted are active influence (pr=.68) and the use of social support (pr=.66). Evasion and passivity are correctly predicted for 64% and 60% of the subjects. *Self-directed* coping behavior is correctly predicted in 67% of the cases (median of pr). Predicting self-blame (pr=.62) seems somewhat more difficult than predicting re-evaluation and palliation (pr=.68), or blaming others (pr=.66). A better prediction ratio seems possible for the relative strength of *stress emotions* in different situations: A total of 76% of the cases are predicted correctly by the situation-behavior theory, with a maximum pr = .86 for depressed feelings, and the lowest prediction ratio occurring for hesitant affect (pr = .68).

Table 12. Lawful prediction ratio of behavior strength in situations of class 1 vs. class 2

	prediction using situation-behavior theory at time 2	prediction of theory conforming behavior from time 1 to time 2
emotional reactions: (mean)	.76	.81
anxious	.74	.86
depressed	.86	.87
aggressive	.70	.76
inhibited	.78	.83
hesitant	.68	.76
abandoned	.78	.79
environment-directed coping behavior: (mean)	.65	.77
evasion/withdrawal	.64	.77
passivity/hesitation	.60	.73
active influence	.68	.80
using social support	.66	.77
self-directed coping behavior: (mean)	.67	.72
palliation	.66	.71
re-evaluation	.68	.74
self-blaming	.62	.78
other-blaming	.68	.71
total (median)	.68	.78

The situation-behavior theory correctly predicts relative behavior strength comparing two kinds of situations with a total mean pr of 68%; in other words, in 68% of the cases our predictions for each individual of our sample were correct using our theory-based assumptions. A prediction ratio of 68% corresponds to an improvement of 36% ((.68-.50)/.50 = .36) in comparison with prediction by chance. Except for passivity, the improvement for all variables is significant (binomial test; Ho: equal probability; one-tailed p < .05).

Another type of prediction, the *prediction by theory and stability*, is given by predicting the behavior which fits the situation-behavior-theory in time 2 of the stress observation record by the corresponding behavior in time 1 which also conforms to the theory.

The results (table 12, 2nd column) show for *environment-directed* coping behavior that 77% of the subjects who behaved in a way which conforms to the theory in time 1 also behaved in that way during time 2. For example, 77% of the subjects who reported, as predicted, evading or avoiding situation 1 more than situation 2 during time 1 also report this difference during time 2. This indicates a relatively high stability over time of the previously mentioned environmental-directed coping efforts - if they conform to the theory. For the *self-directed* and intrapsychic coping efforts the mean proportion of correctly predicted cases is about 72%. Here stability, as it was defined, seems a little lower, but nevertheless it is substantial. Re-evaluation of the stressor's relevance and self-blaming tendency as anticipated by the theory seem to be more consistent (pr=.74 and pr=.78) than palliating stress emotions and blaming others (pr=.71 for both).

Predicting the *emotional reactions* in time 2 from reactions in time 1 seems quite effective, the mean prediction ratio being about pr=.81; i.e. for 81% of the cases prediction of situation-relative emotional strength in time 2 was correct if deduced from emotional behavior in time 1. The best prediction ratio of pr=.87 was reached for feeling depressed (in stressful situations of class 1 vs. class 2), whereas the lowest ratio of correct predictions was achieved for aggressive and hesitant feelings (pr=.76).

For the whole set of self-observation variables, for the different coping efforts as well as for the emotional reactions, a total mean prediction ratio over time of 78% was obtained. This seems a satisfying result with regard to this kind of theory-guided prediction, which specifies relations of behavior tendencies depending on the type of stressful situation as encountered by the subject. The results show *substantial stability* of *theory conform behavior*. This is emphasized by the fact that stability of the behavior strength, which does *not* fit the situation-behavior theory, is very much lower: only about 48% of the cases in time 2 behaved in the same way during time 1; e.g. if someone shows passivity against the prediction of the theory - e.g. passivity in the face of high controllability - then this kind of behavior is less stable from time 1 to time 2.

Additionally, the total of theory-conform environment-directed coping behavior (period 1 and period 2 taken together) is highly correlated with the effectiveness of solving the stressful problem (r=.47;

p < .001). This may serve as a kind of external validation concerning the 'effectiveness' of behavior, which may be more appropriate to this type of predictive theory.

Discussion

Our aim was to compare different types of prediction on the logical and on the empirical level: predictability based on (1.1) general dispositions and (1.2) some more situation-specific but less theory driven assumptions. Both may serve as 'rational' - but 'blind' - predictions by symptoms or indicators. Predictability based on (2.1) theoretical assumptions of situation-behavior-laws, and (2.2) supposing intraindividual stability of the laws, represents another type of prediction.

The results show that the latter approach to behavior prediction is rather encouraging. The best prediction was obtained for stress emotions. This type of behavior may be more predictable because emotions can be interpreted as more automated responses connected with perceptions or appraisals. But it does seem probable that predictability in other kinds of behavior - especially coping efforts - is mediated by cognitive factors such as goals. We conclude that it should be possible to optimize predictability by including such factors in the theoretical structure and empirical analysis.

Case studies III: Assessment in line with the new methods

Thinking back to the scenarios described in the beginning, where Harry is lost and Evelyn has mislaid her earring, what could be expected if Harry and Evelyn were subjects answering S-R-S-R process questionnaire and working with the COMRES over several weeks?

A COMRES-diagnosis of Harry's predicament

Imagine that Harry reported his response, using COMRES after the outcome of his predicament. His rating results concerning his *appraisal of this particular situation* could be as follows: rather high controllability ($=4$), low changeability ($=1$), high negative valence ($=4$), and low probability of reoccurrence ($=1$). For his *emotional response* he may have indicated rather high values for anxiety and aggressiveness, but also for vigorous feelings. He may have reported high values concerning 'active influence' ($=2$) for his *coping effort*, and low values ($=0$) for 'palliation', 'evasion', and 'passivity'. Furthermore he might have stored high values for 'search for information' ($=2$), and for the problem solving success ($=2$). See table 11, left column.

This is one more or less typical example of his stress behavior, recorded using COMRES. This situation comprises one item from sampling his stress behavior but would be insufficient for a diagnosis of his coping tendencies. As described above he would have observed his stress episodes over a period of 4 weeks. After having stored the data relevant to stress and coping behavior in about 40 or 50 stressful events, what kind of diagnostic information would we expect? Firstly we would obtain, at a phenomenological level, an idea about the different *types of stressful events* that Harry experienced during the previous weeks. The sample of daily hassles may consist of problems with his job, with his wife, etc. These could be categorized and put into a rank order taking into account the valence of the events and frequencies of the categories.

What about Harry's stress and coping *tendencies*?

Harry might have appraised controllability of the situations he encountered with a mean of 3.5, which is - compared with our sample of 60
subjects - just beyond the standard deviation of this reference group
(mean $M=2.71$; standard deviation $s=0.58$). His ratings of changeability
may also be rather high, with, say, an average value of 2.0 (reference
group: $M=1.56$, $s=0.57$). These two measures would characterize Harry
as an *optimistic* person who perceives his everyday stressors as more
controllable than does his reference group, but also as optimistic concerning the changeability of stressful situations by their own dynamic.
    Given the above, his mean ratings concerning *emotional reactions*
would be likely to rank in part at the same level as the reference group;
others would be higher. It is possible he could score as follows; 'depres-
sed-serene' 2.61 ($M=2.2$, $s=0.54$), 'anxious-relaxed' 2.7 ($M=2.03$, $s=$
0.54); 'hesitating-spontaneous' 3.2 ($M=2.61$, $s=0.49$), 'lethargic-vigorous'
2.8 ($M=2.66$, $s=0.46$); 'aggressive-peaceful' 2.15 ($M=2.53$, $s=0.52$),
'abandoned-supported' 2.4 ($M=2.10$, $s=0.65$). Compared with the reference group, Harry reacts more spontaneously and is less anxious.

Table 13. Harry's COMRES diagnosis

	Harry's episode example	means of Harry's 42 episodes	reference group M	s
perceived situation characteristics:				
controllability	4	3.5	2.71	0.58
changeability	1	2.0	1.56	0.57
negative valence	4	2.8	2.86	0.61
environment-directed coping behavior:				
active influence	2	1.5	1.03	0.32
evasion/avoidance	0	0.3	0.62	0.31
passivity	0	0.5	0.93	0.31
self-directed coping behavior:				
suppression of information	0	1.2	0.69	0.31
search for information	2	1.4	1.12	0.45
re-evaluation	1	1.2	0.69	0.41
palliation	0	0.8	0.89	0.39
coping efficiency:				
problem solving success	2	1.3	0.97	0.39
real-ideal discrepancy	0	0.4	1.15	0.45

His *coping behavior* may show three conspicuous features; his values for 'suppression of information' high at 1.2 (reference group: M=0.69, s=0.31) as is 'active influence' with 1.5 (M=1.03, s=0.32). His tendency for 'evasion' is low with an average of 0.32 for the total of his observed stressful episodes. Harry's coping style can be described as problem-solving oriented and active, with a tendency to avoid unpleasant thoughts.

He considers the average *success of his coping* attempts as rather high compared to the reference group (=1.3; reference group: M=0.97, s=0.39), and his *causal attributions* for success tend clearly towards internality. Where failure is concerned he is average for both internal and external attribution. So the self-observation data for Harry show him as a person perceiving high self-efficacy and conspicuous internal locus of control.

Table 13 displays some of the above stress and coping variables on three levels: the (fictional) values of the *particular stress episode* - when Harry was lost - the mean values for the *total sample of Harry's* observations (42 episodes), and the means and standard deviations of the *reference group* (see also chapter 4). The extent to which Harry's coping behavior conforms to behavioral rules of adequate coping is analysed in case studies V.

Evelyn's coping tendencies when stressed

The profile of Evelyn's coping attempts may be similar in many respects to the profile built up of Harry when he was lost. We could expect to find a conspicuous tendency for palliation and re-evaluation. She may be more able to adapt to her uncontrollable stressors than Harry and she may be average in instrumental coping. These results could be based on the comparison of her self-observation data with the reference group and on the 'within-analysis' of her rule-oriented behavior (see case studies V).

The stressful episodes in the light of SCPQ diagnosis

Analysis of the Evelyn's responses to the SCPQ questionnaire

The SCPQ questionnaire contains one *hypothetical episode* concerning the loss of a loved object (see appendix, episode no. 4). Evelyn's most interesting responses to that standard stimulus situation might be as follows:

In *appraising the stressful situation*, her rating of controllability at the beginning (just having realized the loss) was rather low, but later (after some unsuccessful efforts to search) it was very low indeed. Her ratings of changeability (e.g. that by chance someone would find the lost object) was very low at the beginning, and also later when loss becomes definite. Evelyn's rating of negative valence might be fairly (not extremely) high during the episode; but having come to terms with the loss, and having re-evaluated the loss of the object and considered its replacement by other things, she might have reduced her rating of negative valence concerning the situation. In the course of the episode her *emotional stress response* turns from rather anxious/nervous feelings into more sad/depressed feelings.

Where her *coping reaction* is concerned, Evelyn first indicated that it would be highly probable for her to react in an active and instrumental way, which she then reduces in the course of the episode. But at the same time, the probability of her staying passive with respect to the stressor (to wait/hesitate) receives a low rating, but increases when the loss becomes unchangeable. She would also increase her subjective probability of re-evaluation (seeing the loss as less important '... there are more important things in life!').

All in all, Evelyn's description of her stress and coping responses in this standard situation of the SCPQ would be quite realistic with regard to her actual behavior in the earring episode. In addition it corresponds to her responses to other SCPQ stimulus episodes. It seems that she knows herself pretty well. Obviously, the quality of such predictions which go from test responses to real stress and coping behavior also depends on the similarity between the hypothetical (model) episodes and real episodes. The content validity and the representation of the stressful stimulus situation is crucial for such references. The more similar the situations, the more valid the reference.

In terms of the test statistics of the SCPQ in relation to population norms and reliability (Reicherts & Perrez, 1991), it is possible to estimate the young lady's 'true value' of her reaction tendencies, e.g. for her *re-evaluation tendency*: her mean test value of 2.60 (mean of all 18 SCPQ episodes) corresponds to a stanine value of 7 (*standard nine* scale), i.e. her tendency is augmented compared with the normal population. Given a reliability of 're-evaluation' of $r_{tt} = .91$, the confidence interval of her true value is situated between 2.30 and 2.90. In other words, with an error level of 5%, Evelyn's re-evaluation tendency is not lower than 2.30 and not higher than 2.90 (which corresponds to the scale levels 'perhaps' to 'probably'). The same assessment procedure of her stress and coping behavior is possible for all other variables of the SCPQ.

Analysis of Harry's SCPQ test result

There is no episode in SCPQ which is as similar to his stressful situation as for Evelyn's loss of the earring. Therefore Harry's SCPQ diagnosis focuses only on his response *tendencies* in the SCPQ questionnaire. His results may almost correspond to the mean value of the normal population; e.g. his tendency to feel anxious (=2.15; stanine = 6), depressed (=2.0; stanine 5) or aggressive (=1.8; stanine = 4). His appraisals of controllability (=2.80; stanine = 6) and of negative valence (=2.85; stanine = 6) are somewhat increased, as is his tendency to actively influence the stressor (=3.15; stanine = 6). The other variables are about average. Emotional reactions, appraisals and active behavior in hypothetical standard situations of the SCPQ when compared to the normal population correspond to the reaction tendencies he reported in the real-life episodes of his COMRES assessment. The combination of the two sources of data - Q-data and self-observation data - allows a more confident diagnosis of his stress behavior.

PART III

APPLICATIONS
IN CLINICAL AND HEALTH PSYCHOLOGY

6. Depressed people coping with aversive situations

Meinrad Perrez and Michael Reicherts

Introduction

Traditional theoretical analysis of etiology proceed from a given psycho-pathological category or syndrome of behavior in order to then explain its origin. In the last decades, an increasing amount of attention has been focused on the process-oriented view of psychopathological phenomena (e.g. Parker, Brown & Blignault, 1986). Certain authors have referred to this point of view as *'performance theory'* (Patterson, 1982) as opposed to the theories of acquisition. In this context we have formulated our inquiry by asking how depressed persons deal with the stress factors of everyday life. In the recent research literature, many references are made to the fact that depressed persons may be characterized by specific types of behavior when coping with their environment, especially when confronted by stressful situations (e.g. Becker, 1981; Blöschl, 1982; Fisher, 1984). Folkman and Lazarus (1986) discussed depression in terms of appraisal and coping. In their study, subjects higher in depressive symptoms appraised stressful events as more stressful, reported more negative emotional reactions, and described their coping behavior by escape-avoidance, accepting responsibility, and self-controlling. These depressive coping behaviors are in contrast with 'anti-depressive activities' (Rippere, 1979; Hautzinger, 1980; Trautmann-Sponsel, 1988). The interpretation of depression as a particular tendency of coping with stressful events - as in Lazarus & Folkman's study - is not to be confused with the interpretation of depression as a global stressor (e.g. Lewinsohn, Antonuccio, Steinmetz & Teri, 1984).

The first section concerning depression, focuses on the *appraisal and coping processes* with *rather controllable aversive and ambiguous situations*. In the second section (see chapter 7), the coping tendencies in situations characterized by loss and failure are analysed. Aversive situations are defined here as the onset of a negative stimulus hurting the person in a psychological or physical sense. In the context of aversive situations ambiguity results in additional threatening cognitions and anxiety. The coping task associated with ambiguity demands a search for information along with palliation as a functional response. In situations of controllable aversiveness with low changeability, a functional response would involve active instrumental behavior. Adequate adaptation presupposes adequate perception of relevant features (e.g. controllability) of the stressor (see chapter 1).

It can be asked if certain specific features of depressive coping behavior emerge more conspicuously during the course of the coping episode than at its beginning. In many respects, depressive persons may react to the beginning of initial stressful situations in a similar way as do nondepressed persons. We assume that some relevant differences may appear later in the course of the episodes - differences which concern the persistence or adaptation of coping behavior. For example, do depressed people persist in their coping efforts in controllable situations which were not successfully influenced by their initial attempts at control? The following study will examine these questions.

Hypotheses

The most important predictions to be tested about depressed vs. nondepressed behavior in face of controllable aversive and ambiguous situations are:

(1.1) Depressed persons perceive and evaluate potential stressors as more stressful, in other words negative valence is increased.

(1.2) They perceive lower controllability and changeability.

(2.1) Environment-directed coping behavior: Depressed individuals exert less influence on the stressor by action, and behave more evasively (e.g. they avoid, withdraw, escape) and/or passively (e.g. they hesitate, become resigned). If the stressful event continues, the depressed individual is less likely to persist in trying to influence the situation.

(2.2) Self-directed coping behavior: Depressed individuals will make a greater effort to palliate their emotions (e.g. emotional discharge) and will search for more (internal) information. They will, however, re-evaluate the stressful situations less. On the other hand, they tend to self-blame, self-reproach, and self-criticize.

(3) In attributing causes to the final outcome of the stressful episodes, the depressed tend toward internal, global, and stable causes to

explain unfavorable outcome. For favorable outcomes they show preference for external, specific, and unstable causes.

Assumptions concerning the process are not described in greater detail.

Method

Research instruments suitable for obtaining a description of the coping processes outlined above have been lacking up to the present time. The available studies concerning depressives single out individual aspects of the process, e.g. characteristics of the cognitive appraisal (tendencies toward distortion; e.g. Lefebvre, 1982; Krantz & Hammen, 1979), or tendencies toward certain causal attributions (Firth & Brewin, 1982; Golin, Sweeney & Schaeffer, 1981; Coyne & Gotlib, 1983). An exception is the study by Folkman and Lazarus (1986), which includes information about primary and secondary appraisals, emotions, and coping behavior comparing stress processes by depressives and nondepressives. In the study described below the process-oriented S-R-S-R-questionnaire (SCPQ) described in chapter 2 was used in its original research version.

The following episodes representing aversive and ambiguous stressful situations were selected from the research version:

- criticism from the partner
- criticism from a colleague
- argument about problems in a relationship
- being charged with a difficult job by the boss
- reproaches by acquaintances about lacking commitment
- reproaches from colleagues about lacking professional commitment

Design and procedure

The study compared the SCPQ process item responses of *two groups*: a group of *depressed subjects* (N=30) and a *matched group of non-depressed normal controls* (N=30). The results reported here refer to the aversive items or episodes mentioned above. The responses represent the beginning (phase 1), the continuation (phase 3), and the outcome (positive and negative) of the stressful episodes. The measures used here are sum scores of the raw values from the 6-point Likert-scales (appraisals and attributions) or of transformed values (1=low; 2=medium; 3=high) according to ratings of subjective probability of the different copings.

Statistical procedures: One-tailed t-test were conducted to test single differences between group means for each phasic variable as predicted by the hypotheses, and F-tests to test the effects of the between-subjects factor (depressed vs. nondepressed group), the within-subjects factors (phase or outcome; repeated measurement), and their interaction.

Subjects

The group of clinically depressed subjects consisted of 22 woman and 8 men (mean age 35.9 years; range: 20 to 62 years). The patients had been placed in psychiatric clinics with a diagnosis of major depression. The group included patients with some reactive components. In addition to the 30 patients, 30 matched non-depressed control individuals were recruited, similar in age, sex, and educational level. In order to control for clinically related characteristics of depression and anxiety, Beck's depression inventory (BDI) and the Spielberger's State-trait-anxiety inventory (STAI) were used as a supplement to the psychiatric diagnosis (see table 14). Both scores are much higher in the depressed group.

Table 14: Sample characteristics and inventory scores of depression and anxiety

group	sex		age	BDI	STAI state	STAI trait
depressed	women	22	M 35.9	M 24.2	M 53.5	M 67.7
	men	8	s 5.0	s 10.6	s 15.3	s 11.8
n = 30			Range 20-62			
non-	women	22	M 36.2	M 5.3	M 33.2	M 48.6
depressed	men	8	s 5.0	s 4.5	s 8.9	s 7.7
n = 30			Range 20-62			

Results

Appraisal

The results (see table 15) fit the hypotheses concerning the appraisals of the potential daily life stressors: The *negative valence*, or strain, rated by the depressed and the normal control group differ significantly ($t=2.02$ and $t=1.70$; $p<.05$) at the beginning of the episode and when stress continues, and for both positive and negative outcome ($t=1.90$ and $t=2.57$; $p<.01$; the difference becomes somewhat greater for the positive outcome). There is no interaction effect between group and process. Further, the depressed people are less hopeful of a positive outcome, as well as perceiving less likelihood of *controllability* and of *changeability*. The differences in appraisals of *controllability* are greater at the beginning of the stressful event ($M=4.37$ vs. 3.83, resp. $M=3.95$ vs. 3.68; $t=-2.90$ and $t=-1.55$; $p<.01$ resp. $p<.10$). The interaction effect between phase and group ($F=5.62$; $p<.05$) indicates different sequential patterns of appraisals: the nondepressed seem to be more 'optimistic' at the beginning, but more adaptive if the stress persists and some efforts to influence the situation may have failed. The *changeability* is also rated lower by the depressed group: the differences are significant both in the beginning and with continued stress. There is no interaction effect of phase and group concerning changeability.

There are significant overall changes for *appraisals during the process*: Controllability is reduced ($M=4.10$ vs. 3.81; $F=25.38$; $p<.001$) and negative valence increased ($M=4.10$ vs. 4.24; $F=5.78$; $p<.05$). Changeability is appraised as constant ($F=0.31$; $p>.10$). The overall differences for perceived negative valence after positive versus negative outcome are very strong ($F=170.55$; $p<.001$).

Environment-directed coping

In its environment-directed coping probabilities (see Table 13) the depressed group exhibits significantly less *active influence* on the situation, i.e. assertiveness toward social stressors at the beginning and continuation of stress ($t=-2.15$ and $t=-2.26$; $p<.05$). Contrary to expectation, however, there is no interaction effect between phase and group which could indicate a lower level persistence by depressed people. But the analysis of type of aversiveness of the situation shows an interaction tendency for the aversive episodes ($n=3$) which are transparent ($F=3.76$; $p=.06$), but not for the ambiguous episodes ($n=3$). This may indicate that lower persistence of the depressives here is revealed only in the assertive resistance to social stressor, but not in active search for information to clarify the meaning of the stressful event. The phenomenon of reduced assertiveness in social situations has recently been addressed with an evolutionary approach by Gilbert (1992). He argues that such inhibition is similar to subordinate behavior in animals.

Table 15: Stress and coping of depressed vs. non-depressed in *aversive situations*

		group depressed		non-depressed		single group diff.	*effects* group	process	process x group
		M	s	M	s	t [1]	F	F	F
appraisals of the situation:									
controllability	beginning	3.83	0.82	4.37	0.61	-2.90^c	5.58^b	25.38^d	5.62^b
	continuation	3.68	0.86	3.95	0.43	-1.55^a			
changeability	beginning	2.29	0.56	2.58	0.72	-1.74^b	4.51^b	0.31	0.30
	continuation	2.22	0.66	2.58	0.63	-2.17^b			
negative valence	beginning	4.27	0.71	3.94	0.54	2.02^b	3.83^a	5.78^b	0.04
	continuation	4.39	0.78	4.09	0.59	1.70^b			
	outcome neg	4.45	0.70	4.13	0.58	1.90^b	8.44^c	170.55^d	0.68
	outcome pos	3.04	0.85	2.54	0.67	2.57^c			
environment-directed coping:									
active influence	beginning	2.64	0.44	2.84	0.28	-2.15^b	5.90^b	6.02^b	0.11
	continuation	2.52	0.49	2.76	0.29	-2.26^b			
evasion	beginning	1.49	0.33	1.33	0.36	1.80^b	4.01^b	9.11^c	0.03
	continuation	1.65	0.47	1.47	0.33	1.69^b			
passivity	beginning	1.67	0.48	1.47	0.36	1.82^b	2.79	1.62	0.50
	continuation	1.69	0.44	1.54	0.41	1.31^a			
self-directed coping:									
search for	beginning	2.59	0.44	2.67	0.32	-0.83	0.26	5.43^b	0.76
information	continuation	2.53	0.45	2.55	0.39	-0.15			
suppression of	beginning	1.37	0.45	1.22	0.31	1.46^a	2.10	0.89	0.15
information	continuation	1.39	0.36	1.29	0.42	1.05			
re-evaluation	beginning	1.84	0.60	2.02	0.48	-1.23	0.49	16.42^d	1.37
	continuation	2.22	0.57	2.22	0.59	-0.04			
palliation	beginning	2.12	0.64	1.81	0.60	1.90^b	3.92^a	0.85	0.00
	continuation	2.07	0.66	1.77	0.58	1.86^b			
self-blaming	beginning	2.06	0.64	1.49	0.34	4.26^d	23.25^d	18.17^d	0.10
	continuation	1.88	0.59	1.28	0.33	4.80^d			
other-blaming	beginning	1.69	0.45	1.61	0.38	0.72	0.00	0.43	3.02^a
	continuation	1.64	0.57	1.72	0.51	-0.60			
causal attribution of outcome:									
external causes	outcome pos.	3.30	0.67	3.28	0.54	0.14	6.03^b	14.04^d	11.63^c
	negative	3.33	0.75	3.99	0.53	-3.90^d			
variable causes	outcome pos.	3.73	0.47	3.77	0.58	-0.33	1.16	0.01	1.85
	negative	3.63	0.68	3.88	0.62	-1.46^a			
global causes	outcome pos.	3.35	0.65	3.88	0.62	0.19	0.35	2.77	4.85^b
	negative	3.38	0.71	3.14	0.77	1.25			

^{a} p<.10; ^{b} p<.05; ^{c} p<.01; ^{d} p<.01; [1] one-tailed

Hence reduced assertiveness would only be seen with those who are regarded as more powerful or superior in some way.

As predicted, the depressed group reports more *withdrawal* or *evasion* (at the beginning and during the episode: t=1.80 resp. 1.69; p<.05) and more passivity (hesitating or resigning behavior; t=1.82 resp. 1.31; p<.05 resp. p<.10).

Taken together, the self-described probabilities of the environment-directed coping behavior demonstrate a consistent and well-known pattern of depressive behavior: less active (assertive), more passive (hesitating and resigning) and more evasive (active avoidance and withdrawal).

There are also overall changes in the different coping behaviors during the episodes indicating the *coping process* (general effect of the phase in repeated measurement): active influence on the stressor is reduced (F=6.02; p<.05) and evasion/avoidance is increased (F=9.11; p<.01). Passivity is only slightly increased and does not yield significance.

Self-directed coping

The predictions about increased search for information and a lower degree of re-evaluation by the depressives are not confirmed by the data (see Table 13). For these intrapsychic coping behaviors there were no differences in comparison to the normal control subjects. As predicted, the depressed group tends to *palliate* their emotions more (t=1.90 and t=1.86; p<.05) and they exhibit significantly more *self-blaming* cognitions (t=4.26 and t=4.80; p<.001). These self-directed coping activities are stronger both at the beginning of and during the stressful episodes. There was no other effect, either by process, or by interaction of group and process. The depressed group reported a slightly stronger tendency to *suppress information* about the stressor at the beginning (t=1.46; p<.10), perhaps as an attempt to protect themselves by shutting out the discomfort. With respect to the other coping tendencies (self-blaming, evasion etc.) however, it doesn't seem a very appropriate cognitive effort in the face of a prevailing controllable situation. There is no difference in the cognitive tendency to *blame others*. There is only a interaction tendency between phase and group (F=3.02; p<.10).

The subjects report changes during the coping process: their probability to re-evaluate is increased, when the aversive stressor remains unchanged (F = 16.42; p < .001), in order to reduce somewhat the search for information (F = 5.42; p < .05), and to reduce self-blaming cognitions (F = 18.17; p < .001). These process characteristics seem plausible in rather controllable situations when aversive social stressors remain unchanged.

Attributions after positive and negative outcome

The depressed group apparently perceives *no difference* between positive or negative outcomes of the situation; the normal control group does (see table 13). As predicted, the nondepressed tend to explain negative outcomes by more *external causes* (t = -3.90; p < .001). The interaction effect due to group and outcome (F = 11.63; p < .01) underlines the different pattern for the internal-external causality dimension. But having been more active (see above), the normals seem to attribute more accurately. This contrasts with some previous results, e.g., from the experimental study of Alloy and Abramson (1979), where nondepressed subjects overestimated their control only in the 'winning' condition, but not in the 'lose' conditions (see also Fisher, 1984). A similar interaction effect (F = 4.85; p < .05) is revealed for the *global-specific* causality dimension. Although the single effects are not significant here, the results do show different trends: the normals exhibit a greater tendency to emphasize specific causes to explain negative outcomes than positive outcomes, whereas the depressed group doesn't distinguish the outcomes. For the *stable-unstable* causality dimension the normal group tend to attribute the negative outcomes more to unstable causes (t = -1.46; p < .10). Only the internal-external dimension, with the two groups taken together, reveals a clear outcome effect (F = 14.04; p < .001); which is due to the difference the normal controls make between coping success and failure.

Discussion

This study compared the S-R-S-R questionnaire responses of a depressed group with those of a matched normal control group. Subjective appraisals of the stressful situations presented in the stimulus episodes, the coping reactions, and causal attributions were analyzed. The statistically significant differences and tendencies found were mostly in the predicted direction. Depressed people appraise such situations as more straining and less controllable than nondepressed people do. They exert less active influence on the aversive controllable stressors and report more evasion and passivity. Differences in the course of the episode appear especially in the appraisal of controllability: the interaction effect between group and process shows the nondepressed to be more adaptive; the depressed people exhibit a kind of rigidity concerning their appraisal of controllability. For most of the other variables the differences between initial reactions hold for the course of the episodes.

Whether this method is capable of differentiating between other clinical groups, as well as sub-groups of depressed, cannot be decided on the basis of this sample. This is somewhat compensated for, however, by the fact that the method employed produces data that confirm construct validity: deficiencies of the depressed, on the levels of cognitive appraisals and subjective probability for coping behaviors, and of causal tendencies. The hypotheses of performance theory are reproduced satisfactorily by this correlational design. Such a design does not, however, permit an interpretation of the possible causal role of these tendencies for the development of depression.

7. Depressed people coping with loss and failure

Michael Reicherts, Sepp Käslin, Fritz Scheurer, Jörg Fleischhauer, and Meinrad Perrez

Introduction

There are many indicators which suggest that situations of *loss and failure* frequently preceded the onset of depression (Holmes & Rahe, 1967; Brown, Bifulco & Harris, 1987). Major critical life events (e.g. divorce, death of a close friend or relative, loss of job) suggest the occurrence of many stressful episodes or sequences of tasks in daily life which are hard to control. However, 'minor' events of loss and failure (e.g. a good neighbour leaves; loss of a loved object), either chronic or recurrent are also hard to cope with. They can disrupt peoples' homeostasis and psychic well-being.

Whereas aversive situations are characterized by the onset of negative conditions or stimuli, *'loss'* can be defined as the abolition of positive conditions (even complex stimuli as provided by a person or a job) and *'failure'* as the non-realization of positive conditions which are expected or probable. Lazarus conceptualizes 'loss' as one basic type of stressful event (Lazarus & Launier, 1978).

A typical objective situation characteristic, which often precedes neurotic depression, is *low controllability* of situations relevant to the person (Seligman 1975; Grant et al., 1981). The loss of a relationship or a job, experiencing separation, failure of important work projects or activities and other uncontrollable and chronic daily stressful events imply such situations. Yet persistent depressive behavior cannot be explained solely in terms of these objective situation characteristics. At best, they explain only transitory depressive reactions, as most people do not respond to events of this type with a lasting depression, unless the uncontrollable stress is stable over time. Attempting to explain individual differences requires the inclusion of cognitive factors. Apparently depressed persons often have defective perceptual tendencies, i.e. cognitive distortions (see Beck 1976, 1991), especially - as indicated by Garber et al. 1980 - defective cognitive tendencies for representing the objective controllability of impairing situations. This restricted perception even applies in situations with a lower level of controllability, leaving limited possibilities for influencing these situations. We would assume therefore, that depressed people appraise their scope for controlling situations of loss and failure less favorably than do nondepressed; in doing so, they show the same tendency as in aversive controllable situations (see chapter 6) (see Fisher, 1984; Folkman & Lazarus, 1986). It would also be expected that they underestimate the fact that certain situations change by themselves, i.e. the aspect of changeability (Perrez 1984). The pattern of causal attributions seems less clear, though there are indications that the depressed are inclined to explain the results of their own actions in an unfavourable way, namely attributing success to external factors and failure to internal and stable factors.

In situations of loss and failure, the typical pattern concerning *the course of coping* during such episodes is also of interest. These questions will be even more important for episodes featuring stressful events which last longer than short-term socially aversive events (see chapter 6). Do depressed people reduce their efforts to prevent loss in the course of the episode if loss becomes definitive? Or, on the other hand, do they intensify their instrumental activities to substitute lost or failed elements and to re-evaluate cognitively what is at stake? The following analysis should also provide an answer to such questions. It should be noted, however, that the assessment and analysis of typical patterns of coping with stress do not allow one to draw conclusions about these patterns being the *cause* or *consequence* of the depressive state.

Hypotheses

Proceeding from the above theoretical perspective, the present study investigates intrapsychic and environment-directed processes with a be- havior regulating function for coping with stressful situations of loss and failure amongst depressed persons. We are particularly interested in the differences in the *perception of situations*, in *coping attempts* and the *causal attributions* between depressed and nondepressed people. The following hypotheses were tested:

(1.1) Depressed people appraise stressful situations of loss and failure as more straining (negative valence is increased).

(1.2) They appraise the controllability and changeability of these situations as lower.

(2.1) Environment-directed coping attempts: In the case of situations of loss and failure depressed people re-orientate themselves less actively towards new sources of reinforcement, and instead try harder to prevent losses which are already occurring. At the same time passive tendencies - hesitating, waiting and resigning - are increased.

(2.2) Self-directed coping attempts: depressed people are more inclined towards palliation (especially in the sense of emotional discharge) and internal search for information. On the other hand, they tend to self-blame. When loss or failure has occurred, they are less likely to suppress information about it and to re-evaluate its relevance.

(3) In the case of a negative outcome of a stressful episode, depressed persons make internal, global and stable causal attributions. A positive outcome is attributed more to external, specific and variable causes.

(4) Assumptions about the appraisal and coping *processes*, from the anticipation phase to the occurrence of loss or failure: the depressed person show a smaller increase for active reorientation and substitution, as well as a smaller decrease in their attempts to prevent the loss although it has virtually occurred.

Method

In this study we used a subset of standardized hypothetical stressful episodes from the S-R-S-R process questionnaire (SCPQ research version) described in chapter 2. The 4 episodes representing situations of loss and failure, which are analysed here, are the following:

- loss of a friendly relationship (a close person moves away)
- loss of a loyal and cooperative work relationship (a colleague leaves)
- failure of a weekend arrangement (a trip to visit someone fails)
- failure of an interesting side job (a side job doesn't work out)

Each of these process items describes an episode consisting of several subsequent phases: the *beginning* of a stressful episode ('anticipation' or 'occurrence'), its *continuation* ('becoming definitive') and the *final outcome* (positive or negative). The response component at the start of and during the episode refers to the appraisal of the situation, the self-directed and environment directed coping behavior and the causal attributions.

The values of the variables are sum scores of the raw values of 6-point Likert-scales for the appraisal of the situation and the causal attribution, and of transformed values (1=low, 2=medium, 3=high) of the ratings of subjective probability of the different coping actions.

Statistical procedures are the same as in the study of coping with aversive episodes: One-tailed t-tests were conducted to test single differences between group means for each variable and phase. F-tests were conducted to test the effects of the between-subjects factor (depressed vs. nondepressed group), the within-subjects factors (phase and outcome of the episode, repeated measurement) and the interactions between process and group or outcome and group.

Subjects

The same people participated as in the study of aversive situations (see chapter 6). A clinical sample of n=30 patients with major depression (n=22 woman, and n=8 men, mean age 35.9) was compared with a matched sample of n=30 nondepressed persons (matched by age, sex and educational level).

Results

Appraisals

The results in table 16 show a higher level overall for depressed people of *subjective impairment* (negative valence) as a result of events of loss and failure presented in the questionnaire. The groups differed significantly both for impending (t=2.23, p<.05) and occurring losses (t=3.02, p<.01), and for positive (t=4.05, p<.001) and negative outcomes (t=3.07, p<.01). The total group effects also proved to be highly significant, while there were no interaction effects between group and phase or group and outcome. For *appraisal of controllability and changeability*, and contrary to the hypothesis, there were no differences in the anticipation phase, where loss or failure is still impending. Differences only appear, when loss or failure actually occur. The depressed persons are less hopeful of a positive change in the situation without any effort on their part - its changeability - (t=-1.99, p<.05) and tend to rate the influence on the situation of their best possible efforts - its controllability - as lower (t=-1.40, p<.10). As expected, belief in the changeability of the looming loss is reduced over the course of the episode (effect of the phase; F=13.92; p<.001). The appraisal of controllability doesn't change over time (F=1.01; p>.10), but it is perceived as lower in situations of loss than in aversive situations. There is also an effect due to the positive vs. negative outcome, which is very marked (F=109.19; p<.001). There are no interaction effects.

Environment-directed coping

At the beginning of the stressful episodes, when loss or failure is only looming, the depressed people hardly differ from the normals in their environment-directed *instrumental coping* tendencies (see table 16). As expected, significant differences only show up when loss or failure become obvious or have become unavoidable (phase 3). The depressed persons are more inclined to try to actively prevent this (t=1.74, p<.05), and they try less than the normals to actively re-orientate themselves to compensate or substitute for loss (t=-3.08, p<.01). The total group effect for the active re-orientation is also significant (t=4.91, p<.05), but not for active prevention. Contrary to our hypotheses, depressed and nondepressed individuals don't differ for subjective probability of passive reactions occurring, such as hesitating at the beginning of loss and failure episodes and in giving up or resigning during their occurrence.

There are strong overall process effects on active prevention, which is reduced (F=25.39; p<.001), and on active substitution or re-orientation, which is augmented (F=32.31; p<.001).

The assumptions concerning the *differential process* of appraisal and coping, which predicted the lower adaption of the depressed, are supported by the significant interaction effect between process and group for active reorientation (F=4.67; p<.05) and by the interaction tendency for active prevention (F=3.76; p<.10): Accordingly, it seems the depressed are less likely to adapt by withdrawing their attempts at prevention and instead intensifying their efforts at re-orientation and substitution for situations of loss. This is underlined by the tendency of the depressed to extreme and inappropriate ('highly active') attempts to prevent loss and failure ('by all means', 'at all costs'), which aren't described here in detail.

Table 16. Stress and coping of depressed vs. non-depressed in *loss/failure situations*

		group depressed		non-depressed		single group diff.	effects group	process	process x group
		M	s	M	s	t [1]	F	F	F
appraisals of the situation:									
controllability	beginning	3.79	0.75	3.93	0.81	-0.66	1.23	1.01	1.01
	continuation	3.64	0.78	3.93	0.79	-1.40[a]			
changeability	beginning	2.63	0.75	2.89	0.89	-1.26[b]	2.94[a]	13.92[d]	0.67
	continuation	2.30	0.73	2.68	0.76	-1.99[b]			
negative valence	beginning	3.65	0.67	3.28	0.62	2.23[b]	8.44[c]	0.01	0.87
	continuation	3.73	0.72	3.22	0.58	3.02[c]			
	outcome neg	3.92	0.70	3.38	0.67	3.07[c]	17.37[d]	109.19[d]	0.68
	outcome pos	3.04	0.70	2.35	0.62	4.05[d]			
environment-directed coping:									
active prevention	beginning	2.20	0.54	2.24	0.47	-0.32	0.60	25.39[d]	3.76[a]
	continuation	2.00	0.55	1.79	0.36	-1.74[b]			
active substitut.	beginning	2.06	0.53	2.21	0.52	-1.10	4.91[b]	32.31[d]	4.67[b]
	continuation	2.24	0.55	2.62	0.38	-3.08[c]			
passivity	beginning	1.73	0.48	1.78	0.51	0.46	0.00	2.19	0.65
	continuation	1.69	0.44	1.54	0.41	1.31[a]			
self-directed coping:									
search for	beginning	2.51	0.54	2.54	0.46	-0.25	0.19	18.67[d]	2.07
information	continuation	2.33	0.55	2.19	0.52	0.98			
suppression of	beginning	1.37	0.53	1.26	0.34	1.14	0.08	12.38[d]	5.07[b]
information	continuation	1.44	0.52	1.60	0.55	-1.34[a]			
re-evaluation	beginning	2.36	0.53	2.47	0.52	-0.88	2.11	2.88[a]	0.31
	continuation	2.43	0.55	2.62	0.47	-1.55[a]			
palliation	beginning	1.93	0.48	1.68	0.56	1.61[a]	3.61[a]	0.21	0.37
	continuation	1.98	0.65	1.67	0.60	1.95[b]			
self-blaming	beginning	1.74	0.55	1.35	0.40	3.16[c]	17.95[d]	9.29[c]	0.49
	continuation	1.62	0.52	1.15	0.22	4.49[d]			
other-blaming	beginning	1.43	0.45	1.34	0.33	0.90	1.77	0.23	0.46
	continuation	1.48	0.41	1.33	0.36	1.51[a]			
causal attribution of outcome:									
external causes	outcome pos.	3.63	0.63	3.73	0.79	-0.59	2.00	23.80[d]	2.22
	negative	3.90	0.72	4.25	0.66	-1.96[b]			
variable causes	outcome pos.	3.59	0.62	3.57	0.77	0.14	0.09	0.04	0.90
	negative	3.53	0.70	3.66	0.71	-0.69			
global causes	outcome pos.	3.05	0.68	3.26	0.88	-1.03	0.04	1.96	10.91[d]
	negative	3.19	0.67	2.91	0.86	1.42[a]			

[a] $p < .10$; [b] $p < .05$; [c] $p < .01$; [d] $p < .01$; [1] one-tailed

Self-directed coping

No differences were found with regard to *internal search for information*, (see table 16). The assumption that an increased search for information would be undertaken by the depressed subjects is therefore not confirmed. Yet it has to be noted that the present description of behavior is aimed at internal activities and does not include search for information. As expected, the normals demonstrate a stronger tendency to *suppress information* (t=-1.34; p<.10) when loss occurs, whereas the depressed have slightly higher, yet not significantly different values when it is looming. A significant interaction effect (F=5.07; p<.05) occurs as a result of differences in the course of the episodes. This again indicates the higher adaptability of the normals, because when loss or failure has occurred or is unavoidable, an increased (but not too dominant) tendency to fade out, switch off etc. seems to be quite appropriate in the face of an event that can hardly be influenced.

Nondepressed people show a tendency (t=-1.55; p<.10) to *re-evaluate* a situation as a means of coping. Yet the interaction effect is not significant here. With search for information, suppression of information and re-evaluation, the group total effects are not significant. The inclination towards *palliation* - the attempt to directly influence one's own emotions by smoothing and calming them - is higher in depressed persons than in normals; they report higher subjective probabilities for impending (t=1.61; p<.10) and for occurring stress (t=1.95; p<.05).

As expected, the tendency towards *self-blame* as an intrapunitive form of coping is clearly increased in the depressed group. It is sometimes characterized as 'taking responsibility' (cf. the study of Folkman & Lazarus, 1986). The difference is highly significant both in impending (t=3.16; p<.01) and presently occurring situations (t=4.49; p<.001). Accordingly the group total effect is F=17.95; p<.001. There are no interaction effects between group and phase for both palliation and self-reproaches. *Other-blaming* (internal) is only slightly augmented when episodes of loss continue (t=1.51; p<.10). The global change of self-directed coping attempts during the episodes is illustrated by reduced search for information (F=18.67; p<.001), intensified suppression of information (F=12.38; p<.001) and re-evaluation (F=2.88; p<.10). Also self-blaming tendencies are weakened (F=9.19; p<.01) when loss and failure become a fact (in spite of the prevention) - as the stimulus episodes suggest.

Causal attributions

As expected, depressed persons are relatively more inclined than the normals to locate the causes for an unfavorable outcome of loss/failure episodes within themselves ($t = -1.96$; $p < .05$; see table 16). Yet the reverse effect cannot be found for a favourable outcome; there is virtually no difference here: both groups locate the causes around the middle of the *internal-external attribution* dimension. Neither the group total effect nor the interaction effect is significant. For attributions of *global vs. specific* causes a different tendency is found only for unfavourable outcomes ($t = 1.42$; $p < .10$). Depressed individuals are more likely to attribute unfavorable outcomes to global causes rather than to specific causes, which may, however, only be characteristic for single situations. Thus, a highly significant interaction effect can be found ($F = 10.91$; $p < .001$) which is compatible with the diverging attributions between positive and negative outcomes and the reversed attribution direction of depressed people and normals. None of the expected differences could be found for the attributional dimension of *unstable vs. stable* causes.

On the whole, the responses to the questionnaire show a quite consistent picture of how depressed persons deal with everyday loss and failure situations over time.

At the beginning of the episodes, during the so-called anticipation phase, when loss or failure are impending with a certain probability, the depressed can hardly be distinguished from the nondepressed. However, depressed individuals at first perceive the situation as more impairing and are more inclined towards palliation and especially towards self-reproaches and self-blame, e.g. for having contributed towards the generation of these situations. In the course of the test episodes, though, when loss or failure occurs or is imminent and hardly avoidable, there are typical differences: Depressed persons not only perceive the situation as more stressful, they also perceive the changeability and controllability of the situations and thus the 'gross'-hope for a positive outcome as lower. Yet at the same time they try harder than the nondepressed do to prevent loss or failure, but try less to actively re-orientate themselves. They try less to suppress information and to reappraise the situation, but are rather more likely to try to directly influence their unpleasant emotions. Self-blame and intrapunitive tendencies continue. Typical differences concerning the process become apparent in the higher adaptability of the nondepressed persons for instrumental coping attempts and in the suppression of information.

Discriminant analyses

For a first evaluation of the power of the variables of the S-R-S-R questionnaire to discriminate between depressed and nondepressed persons, different discriminant analysis were conducted, in spite of the small samples. The contribution of the various variables described here in discriminating between the depressed and the nondepressed group was evaluated.

It was possible in 95% of cases to discriminate between the depressed and nondepressed group, when only the variables of the 4 loss and failure episodes were included in analysis. A similar result occurred on the basis of aversive and ambiguous situations, as analysed in chapter 6. Omitting the fact that there are 4 loss/failure episodes versus 6 aversive episodes, aggregated in the variables (loss/failure episodes are therefore more economic), both types of stressors can be considered as equally relevant to depressive behavior. A comparison of the contribution of the different phases of the questionnaire episodes towards the discrimination of the groups revealed for the beginning of an episode a level of discrimination of 95%, and for the continuation and the outcome a discrimination of 100%. That is to say that the assessment of the later responses in imagined sequences of everyday stressors seems to be at least as effective as the responses at the beginning of such episodes.

In another discriminant analysis, the *patients* who had *reactive components* in their symptomatology were analysed separately from the patients with 'pure' major depression. Because of the low number of subjects, this analysis had only an exploratory function. It produced a 100% discrimination of the three groups, the nondepressed (N=30), the 'pure' major depressed (N=20) and the patient with major depression containing reactive components (N=10). It was striking that for most variables the group mean values of the 'reactive' subgroup were more clearly in the direction of the hypotheses than those of the 'pure' subgroup. This indicates the possibility of differentiating clinical subgroups of depression on the basis of the psychological concepts outlined here. For differential diagnostics it has to be noted that this procedure was not specifically developed in order to differentiate clinical disorders but to furnish intervention-relevant information about coping with everyday stress. Findings about the differentiation of clinical groups are to be considered mainly as indices for the validity of the theoretical and methodological premises of this approach.

Discussion

The questionnaire responses of the depressed, concerning how they deal with everyday stressors, were compared to those of the nondepressed control subjects. Appraisals of the situation, internal and external coping attempts and causal attributions were assessed in the course of S-R-S-R tasks concerning situations of loss and failure. Statistically significant differences occurred which were as predicted.

The *environment-directed* coping behavior of the depressed is characterized by increased attempts to prevent losses and failure and a decreased tendency to re-orientate and to substitute sources of reinforcers. In aversive situations their coping behavior was characterized by withdrawal, evasion and exerting less influence. *Self-directed* coping attempts tend to be characterized by self-reproach and increased palliation, and, when losses have occurred, a tendency to less actively suppress information about them and to re-evaluate them to a lesser extent.

Similarly, *appraisal* of the situation is characterized by predicted differences between the depressed and the nondepressed control group. Generally depressed demonstrate higher strain and lower changeability of the loss events and a lesser belief for controllability of aversive events. For causal attribution, the depressed emphasize internal causes for negative outcome of the episodes. On the other hand, the assumptions about passivity of the depressed to loss and failure and about a generally increased search for information were not confirmed.

With regard to *differences over the course* of the episode (specific interaction effects of group and process) it was revealed that depressed people seem to be less adaptive towards episodes of loss and failure. They don't adjust their active re-orientation and their suppression of unpleasant information concerning those situations presented in the process questionnaire.

Single assumptions about the appraisal of situations and about attribution tendencies, especially in loss and failure, were only partly confirmed. To what extent this is due to the procedure involved and its implementation, and to what extent there is internal validity with this method cannot be decided on the basis of this sample. The results have to be validated by way of tests on further clinical groups and subgroups. The comparison between the nondepressed control group and another sample of nondepressed 'normals' (N=65), which were recruited for the test analysis, shows a good concordance in most variables.

The features of depressive coping behavior should not be seen as causal factors for the development of major depression. Coping by depressed people may be considered as a defining element of depression (e.g. passivity) on a phenomenological level, or as sustaining factor of depressive behavior and emotion (e.g. underestimation of controllability --> evasion --> failure --> depressed feeling). In both cases their assessment includes practical possibilities for intervention. Coping deficits of depressed people can be subject to psychological intervention (see, for example, the coping training developed by Lewinsohn et al., 1984). Stimulus material of the type described here could serve as hypothetical standard situations for coping training in guided imagery (e.g. Hänggi & Schedle, 1987).

Likewise, it cannot be decided on the basis of the samples described above whether this procedure is able also to differentiate between other clinical groups. This weakness is alleviated by the fact that the procedure obviously yields construct validity and records theoretically coherent deficits which are typical of depressed persons at the level of subjective perceptions of a situation and of the subjective probability of coping and attributional tendencies. The results reported here supplement those concerning the reactions of depressed persons to aversive and ambiguous situations in a way which is theoretically consistent with previous related work (see chapter 6).

8. HIV-infection and stress:
Buffering effects of coping behavior and its treatment

Meinrad Perrez, Michael Reicherts and Bernard Plancherel

Introduction

The question of how people cope with the stress of knowing they have AIDS is of considerable psychological importance. To become conscious of having AIDS causes an emotional and cognitive pattern characterized by the highest possible insecurity, threat and anxiety. To become conscious of one's condition at a later stage of the process, at the stage of full-blown AIDS, is similar to an awareness of a certain death or a capital sentence. Concerned people are worried about social inconveniences, their inattention in sexual behavior, what caused the infection etc.. The HIV-drama is, in the experience of affected people, not a tragedy of virus and immunosuppressors, but is a tragedy of psychological functioning agents such as anxiety, loss of one's job or loved ones, aggression and solitude. It can be assumed, however, that the intensity of mental misery may be buffered by coping tendencies.

The main topics of psychological research in this new area concern (1) the identification of the important types of stressors which require relevant lifestyle adaptation for HIV-positive people, (2) the ways of coping or adaptation manifested by HIV-infected people, and (3) the effects of coping styles on psychological features like well being, anxiety etc..

The main stressor which is deeply disturbing the homeostasis of HIV-infected people is, *at the beginning*, the *message of the diagnosis*. Most people react with shock, depressive feelings and fear (Frigo et al., 1986; Morin & Batchelor, 1984). Drug addicts seem to react to the same message in a less intensive way (Casadontes et al., 1986). The second type of important stressors are the *social problems* resulting from public knowledge of the threatening diagnosis, including the threat of loss of one's job (Tross & Hirsch, 1988; Jäger, 1988). In opposition to this threat, however, is the fact that communication of the diagnosis to relevant people is often experienced as helpful (Coates et al., 1987). In this context we have to consider also the problem of 'coming out' of the homosexuals (Nichols, 1985; Coates et al., 1987). A third problem consists of the adaptation of behavior to a *new healthy life-style* such as stopping smoking, more healthy eating etc., including the change of sexual risk behavior, which reduces the risk of health deterioration or the risk of infection. For a majority this is associated with changing well established behavior patterns (Joseph et al., 1985) which can be costly in psychological terms (Ostrow et al., 1985).

One to two years after diagnosis, in a Swiss sample (N=40) of HIV-infected male homosexuals, 72 % displayed moderate to high apprehension about falling ill, 58 % felt depressed when thinking about threatening illnesses, and 48% expressed high anxiety about dying. 45 % had problems with 'coming out'.

During a *later phase*, anxiety due to the AIDS-related complex becomes predominant for many patients (Tross et al., 1986). Chuang (1989) compared psychological distress and well-being across three groups: homosexual and bisexual male patients diagnosed as having asymptomatic HIV-infection (N=24), AIDS-related complex (N=22), or AIDS (N=19): 'Patients with asymptomatic HIV-infection and AIDS-related complex showed significantly greater levels of depressive symptoms, more disturbance, and trait anxiety than did patients with AIDS' (Chuang et al., 1989, 878). This study has not confirmed the results of Cohen and Weisman (1986), who found that people with AIDS showed different types of psychic distortions like major depression, reactive depression, borderline problems, bereavement etc.

All of these different problems of which there are many, require some adaptation.

What is actually known about the ways in which HIV-positive people cope? Klauer, Ferring and Filipp (1989) analysed the way in which HIV-positive people cope with their stress in comparison with cancer and rheumatism patients. HIV-positive persons are characterized by their preoccupation with searching for information. Like the cancer patients, they often reacted by 'ruminating' and estimated the efficiency of their coping as rather low. Chevrier (1987) studied the coping of 24 young HIV-positives (18 males and 6 females) in a German city by way of in-depth interview. The majority (N=14) deliberately invested in changing their health-related behavior regarding nutrition, sporting activities and regular contact with a physician. 18 subjects undertook an intensive search for information about their infection by consulting the physician, or reading books or journals on AIDS. The others avoided thinking about the problem as far as possible.

There are only a few studies dealing with the relationship between *coping styles and their effects* on psychological factors for HIV-positive people. All the studies carried out thus far have utilized a correlational design. Schiefer-Hofmann (1986) found substantial correlations between *emotion-centered* coping and trait anxiety and a negative correlation between the same coping tendency and psychosomatic symptoms. *Problem-centered coping* is significantly correlated with mental health-indicators.

Namir et al. (1987) studied the coping tendencies and psychological characteristics of 50 homosexual AIDS-patients who have recently fallen ill. 85% of the patients undertook an intensive information search, 80% deliberately tried to change their behavior towards a healthier lifestyle. *Cognitive avoidance* was observed rather rarely. But those who preferred cognitive avoidance were more strongly psychologically disturbed than the group with active problem solving coping strategies, including seeking social support. The group who centered on problem-solving exhibited higher self-esteem and lower depression scores.

Figure 8: Analysis of the effects of coping tendencies moderating the association between HIV-related stressors and psychological well-being

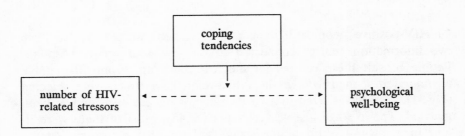

The following study focuses on the relationship between coping characteristics of HIV-positives and their psychological well-being. Billings and Moos (1981) found some evidence that specific coping responses moderated the relationship between stressful events and measures of negative

mood. We assume in the same sense that the relationship between HIV-related everyday stressors and indicators of psychological well-being are influenced by coping tendencies (as depicted in figure 8). We first compare stress and coping behavior of HIV-positives with normal control subjects. Following this we address the question of whether there are coping tendencies which moderate the relationship between the experience of stress and psychological well-being of HIV-infected people. In the last part the results of an intervention program to improve the coping tendencies of HIV-positive persons is described.

Hypotheses

(1) The correlation between HIV-related stressful experience with measures of anxiety and depression may be strengthened by
(1.1) omitting palliative coping efforts,
(1.2) a tendency to self-blame in stressful situations, and
(1.3) a tendency to evade/avoid or stay passive - instead of instrumental behavior - in controllable situations.
(2) The tendencies for coping with stress of HIV-positives can be improved through a training program.

Methods

Sample

40 HIV-positive people (38 men and 2 women) were recruited from two information centres connected to two Swiss university hospitals. People consult these centres for medical check up. From this sample all *homosexual* men *without* the AIDS-related syndrome were selected (N=31). 15 subjects lived in a relationship; 4 people were or had been married. The average age was 37 years (28;48). Most of them were living in a town. A third of the group had a higher education. At the time of the psychological inquiry all subjects worked full or part-time.

Assessment methods and treatment

The *assessment of HIV-related stressors* and *coping tendencies* comprised an interview and two questionnaires. We constructed a S-R-question-naire (SCPQ-HIV) with a similar structure to the questionnaire described in chapter 2, but with only one S-R sequence. The hypothetical HIV-related stressful situations were collected by previous interviews with HIV-positives. 12 prototypical situations were worked out or selected as a situation sample for different coping tasks: for aversive situations and for situations characterized by loss. Three hypothetical situations were transferred from the original SCPQ-questionnaire (episodes 2, 12, and 15, see appendix). The response variables (ratings) concerned stressor appraisal variables, goals, and reaction variables. *Appraisals* include controllability, changeability, and valence of the stressful situations. Familiarity refers to the frequency of the subject meeting this kind of stressor since diagnosed as being HIV-positive. The total sum of the rated frequencies over the 12 situations serves as indicator for the amount of experienced stressful events (see below). *Reaction variables* of the SCPQ-HIV questionnaire are the same as in the original SCPQ questionnaire (see chapter 2) and concern emotional reactions to the imagined stressful situations, and the subjective probability for self-directed and environment-directed coping efforts.

The second questionnaire was an situation-free inventory about *coping with illness* (FEKB; Klauer & Filipp, 1987)). The patient is required to estimate his frequencies for 64 different coping responses which are related to 5 coping dimensions. The dimensions were extracted by factor analysis: 'rumination', 'search for social belonging', 'defense from threat', 'search for information' and 'search for support in religion'.

Measures of state anxiety and depression were used to measure *negative indicators for mental well-being*. Anxiety was measured using Spielberger's State-Trait-Anxiety Inventory (Laux, Glanzmann, Schaffner and Spielberger, 1981) and depression using Beck's depression inventory (BDI).

The *intervention study* was carried out within the same sample. The subjects were invited to participate in a psychological program to improve their coping competencies. At the time of writing n=21 subjects from the initial sample of N=31 gay men have finished the whole longitudinal study. 9 of them decided to attend the training (see below); those subjects who did not participate in the program but were involved in the study for over a year, formed the control group (n=12). The treatment group had higher values for all negative psychological indicators in comparison to the control group. This was a predictable effect of the recruitment strategy. The group differences for the pre-measurements had to be controlled for by statistical procedures (analysis of covariance). All subjects were *re-assessed* three times at 4-monthly intervals, i.e. over one year. The re-assessments included questionnaires on coping tendencies and other psychological features relevant for coping and self-observation.

The *training program* was intended to improve *general coping competencies* by behavioral training and client-centered counselling sessions. The specific treatment goals were (i) to treat anxiety by improvement of palliative competence (especially relaxation), (ii) to improve ability to cope in a active and instrumental way in controllable situations, and (iii) to improve health behavior (sexual, nutritional). Every participant could attend between 25 and 30 sessions.

Results

Validity of the SCPQ-HIV questionnaire

The SCPQ-HIV questionnaire was compared with the FEKB questionnaire of Klauer and Filipp (1987) which aims to measure similar psychological constructs. The SCPQ-HIV variables were correlated to the 5 FEKB-scales ('rumination', 'search for social belonging', 'defense of threat', 'search for information' and 'search for support in religion'). The most interesting correlations were as follows (all significant at the $p < .05$ level): the SCPQ-variable 'suppression of information' was negatively correlated with FEKB-'search for information' ($r = -.40$) and 'search for social belonging' ($r = -.44$). SCPQ-variable 'self-blame' and 'blaming others' was associated with FEKB-'rumination' ($r = .42$ and $r = .44$). Also correlated was SCPQ-'palliation' ($r = .37$), which also correlated to FEKB-'cognitive avoidance'. Interestingly, *environment-directed* coping tendencies in the SCPQ-HIV showed a clear correlation pattern with the FEKB-scales; 'active influence' on stressor was positively correlated with FEKB-'search for information', 'defense of threat', and 'search for social belonging' ($r = .35$, $r = .31$ and $r = .35$) and negatively with FEKB-'rumination' ($r = -.38$). SCPQ-'passivity' (tendency to hesitate, resign) had just the inverse pattern, and SCPQ-'evasion' (tendency to escape, avoid) was clearly correlated with FEKB-'rumination' ($r = .50$). Even if not all correlations reach a substantial level, there is no correlation in opposition to what would be expected. The results indicate that this variant of the SCPQ - adapted for HIV-positive subjects - produce interpretable findings concerning psychological features of coping with stressful situations by this particular group.

Comparing stress and coping behavior of HIV-positives with normal control subjects

A second analysis was conducted to look for differences in stress and coping tendencies between the HIV-positives and 50 people from the SCPQ norm group sample. This comparison was possible concerning the three stressful situations which are the same in the original SCPQ-questionnaire. There are only a few differences between the HIV-group and the norm group. The HIV-group describes *stronger intentions to emotional equilibration* and in particular to equilibration of *self-esteem*, and they report more *suppression of information* and *re-evaluation* in the situations of the questionnaire. There is also a somewhat stronger tendency for the HIV-positives *to stay passive*. The appraisal of situations, emotional reactions and other coping behaviors are very similar to that of the reference group.

Coping tendencies as moderators

Analysis of the moderating effects of coping tendencies on the relation between HIV-related stressors and psychic well-being was conducted as follows. The *amount of HIV-related stressors* the subjects had experienced since their diagnosis is operationalized by the frequency with which they encountered the stressful situations, i.e. their familiarity with the hypothetical situations in the SCPQ-HIV questionnaire (see above). This indicator was at first correlated with measures of anxiety and depression.

Analysing the influence of variables on the relation of independent (x) and dependent (y) variables, usually two types of variables are distinguished: moderator variables and mediating variables. 'Moderators' concern presuppositions or general conditions for the relation between variable x and variable y; they do not represent the process mechanism in a strong sense. On the other hand 'mediators' concern the mechanism which explains the influence of x on y. We consider in our study coping tendencies as trait-like conditions which buffer the link between stressors and psychic well being. More generally, features we interpret them as moderator variables. The methodological and statistical questions are distinguishable from this theoretical question, if the hypothesis concerning buffering is empirically analysed.

The coefficients of correlations are compared in the study. This is a simple procedure, containing some problems (cf. Baron & Kenny, 1986). The method should be applied only if homogeneity of variance of the variables of the two subgroups is assured. Furthermore, the amount of measurement error in the dependent variable should not vary as a function of the moderator. The data of our study meet the criteria of the first condition (F-tests). The second condition is difficult to test. However, the effects of an overestimation of the difference between correlations, caused by differences in the variances, can be considered as less important, if the analysis is testing a hypothesis. The applied procedure may be appropriate in consideration of the small sample, even if the above-mentioned problem exists. The applied critical ratio corrects deviations of the small samples which are caused by the odd number of 31 subjects or by the separation of the two subgroups by the medians.

The *global correlation* between HIV-stressors and indicators of psychic well-being allows an indication of their overall association: Depression (BDI) is significantly correlated with the number of stressors ($r = .38$; $p < .05$), as is a trend towards state anxiety ($r = .26$, $p < .10$).

Table 17. Correlations between HIV-specific stressors (frequency) and mental health (state anxiety STAI and depression BDI) moderated by coping tendencies (low vs. high) in the SCPQ-HIV questionnaire (n=16 vs. n=15)

correlation between	stressors and *anxiety* when coping tendency			stressors and *depression* when coping tendency		
	low	high	diff. $r_{low}-r_{high}$	low	high	diff. $r_{low}-r_{high}$
self-directed coping:						
search for information	.35	.25	0.28	.19	.39	0.55
suppression of information	.44	-.02	1.23	.61	.03	1.70[b]
re-evaluation	.07	.48	1.13	-.23	.74	2.95[c]
palliation	.54	-.51	2.91[d]	.46	.12	0.98
self-blaming	-.37	.61	2.75[c]	-.34	.52	2.32[b]
other-blaming	-.40	.73	3.40[d]	-.42	.55	2.67[b]
environment-directed coping: *aversive situations:*						
active influence on stressor	.35	-.10	1.18	.40	.27	0.36
evasion/avoidance	-.10	.52	1.70[b]	.08	.54	1.31[a]
passivity	-.35	.63	2.78[c]	.25	.42	0.47
loss and failure:						
active influence on stressor	.37	.03	0.90	.34	.48	0.43
active re-orientation	.36	.01	0.93	.43	.32	0.32
passivity	-.07	.69	2.30[b]	.11	.64	1.62[a]

[a] $p < .10$; [b] $p < .05$; [c] $p < .01$; [d] $p < .01$; [1] one-tailed

To study the *moderating effect* of different coping tendencies, median values were used to separate subjects who demonstrated low and high probabilities of given coping categories. Correlation coefficients were then calculated separately for the two groups, and their difference was compared using the critical ratio of the transformed coefficients according to Fisher.

If there is a statistically significant difference between the correlation coefficients in the two coping subsamples, it may be interpreted as evidence for a moderating effect of the particular coping tendency.

This analysis revealed the following *moderating effects of coping* on the relation between stress and well-being (table 17):

There is a moderating influence on *anxiety* of (a) palliation which seems to 'buffer' the impact of stress, of (b) self- and other-blaming which seem to reinforce its impact, and (c) also for evasion/avoidance and passivity in stressful but controllable situations which also seem to reinforce state anxiety.

The study reveals a moderating effect on *depression* of (a) suppression of information which seems to 'buffer' the relation between stressors and depression, (b) of self- and other-blaming and of re-evaluation strengthening the impact of stressors, and (c) also a tendency for evasion and passivity to 'reinforce' depression.

All results are as predicted, except for the fact that re-evaluation seems to 'strengthen' the impact of HIV-related stressors on depression.

First results concerning the treatment of coping tendencies

The following table 18 shows the first results concerning coping competence from 4 assessments over a period of 12 months. The 9 subjects in the treatment group were compared using a repeated measures variance analysis with the 12 subjects in the control group. The SCPQ-HIV questionnaire was used as an instrument to measure the effects of the treatment. We conducted an 2x4 repeated measures analysis of variance/ covariance (using treatment vs. control as between group factor and time - the 4 measures - as within-group factor; the 1st measurement was controlled as covariate). The interaction effects between group and time indicate treatment effects.

The results in table 18 reveal a significant decrease in distress *(negative valence)* over time for the therapy group compared with the control group (interaction effect between group and time $F = 2.97$; $p < .04$). The treatment group learned to appraise self-threatening situations in a less stressful way.

There was also a tendency for the therapy group to increase *active coping* attempts over time ($F = 2.07$; $p < .12$), and a tendency to decrease *evasive* behavior (withdrawal, avoidance) in stressful, but controllable situations ($F = 2.60$; $p < .07$). Whereas the control group, without training, did not demonstrate comparable changes for the probability of coping behaviors. The treatment group learned to actively influence controllable aversive situations instead of avoiding or being passive, which is characteristic of depressive people. All in all the results suggest that it is possible to change coping tendencies of HIV-positives by a counseling program which contains elements of behavior training.

Table 18. Changes in HIV stress and coping behavior: treatment ($n = 9$) vs. control ($n = 12$) group of HIV-infected people

SCPQ-HIV variables	month	0	4	8	12	group x time interaction p
negative valence	treatment	2.81	2.42	2.38	2.11	
	control	2.68	2.76	2.69	2.58	.011
active influence on stressor	treatment	2.13	2.58	2.49	2.46	
	control	2.96	2.77	2.82	3.02	.115
evasion (withdraw/avoid)	treatment	1.79	1.41	1.39	1.49	
	control	1.23	1.27	1.33	1.31	.061

Discussion

It was postulated that being HIV-positive would have low predictive value for psychic well-being. It was assumed that certain features of coping tendencies were better explanations of psychic well-being. Mental misery or well-being obviously results from different sources of variance. One source may be the experience of HIV-infection as a *critical life event* demanding high effort to re-adapt. Another may be the extent of *social support*.

The importance of *tendencies to cope* with stressful events as an important causal factor for well-being was considered. Critical life events are not abstract and homogeneous entities, suitable as units for psychological analysis; rather they engender a variety of different micro-stressors, interfering in various ways with daily life in the form of real life micro-episodes which are more or less stressful. These episodes can be psychologically analysed. In our questionnaire they are represented as S-R-sequences, consisting of hypothetical stressful situations, and as appraisal and coping responses. We formulated hypotheses about the moderating effect of some coping characteristics on indicators of psychic well being. Furthermore we postulated that it will be possible to improve the coping tendencies (competencies) by a training.

The results of this study confirm the hypotheses with one exception (re-evaluation) and meet the results of other studies with normal as well as with depressed people (see chapters 3, 6, and 7). To cope in an active way in controllable stressful situations, to cope by palliation - using their efficient variants - in emotionally aversive situations, and to reduce passive and avoidant behavior, - these tendencies seem to buffer the impact of stressful events on depression and anxiety, which can be considered as negative indicators of mental health. We found with the HIV-positive group a global correlation between the frequency of HIV-related stressful daily events and depression and anxiety. A further within-group analysis - dividing the sample into groups with high and low tendencies for different coping categories - shows that the connection between stressors and psychic well being is moderated by coping tendencies. As intrapersonal resources they can mitigate the psychological impact of HIV-related everyday stressors.

The intervention study suggests that it is possible to influence the coping style of HIV-positive people. The treatment sample is probably not representative for HIV-positive gay men. But the subjects in our study may be typical for Swiss gay men suffering from being HIV-positive and motivated to attend health behavior training. Further analyses of the data are required to show if the change of the coping tendencies actually enhances the mental well-being and buffers the experience of stress. The results concerning the change of distress in HIV-related situations - measured by the SCPQ-HIV questionnaire - can be interpreted as an indicator for such an improvement. The intention of the treatment study was to explore if coping behaviors can be changed. Obviously, without a different treatment control group no conclusions about the specifity of this particular treatment can be made.

The results underline the relationship between coping behavior and mental health. Beyond changing nutritional and sexual behavior, the improvement of dealing better with daily stressful situations is revealed as being related to health: Mastering daily stressful events can have effects on the quality of life as well on the course of the illness, and probably on the immune system.

9. Mental health and coping with everyday stressors

Meinrad Perrez

Introduction

The relationship between mental health and coping with stress has been discussed repeatedly in previous years (Folkman & Lazarus, 1982; Folkman, Lazarus, Gruen & DeLongis, 1986; DeLongis, Lazarus & Folkman, 1988; Weber & Laux, 1990). Mental health has been considered as a more or less stable state as continuous affective well-being, consisting of several components such as will power, adaptability, self-assurance etc. (Becker, 1984a, 1986). Mental health has also been defined as the ability to cope successfully with external and internal demands (also Becker, 1986). Yet we may ask just what does 'successful coping' mean - and in what way is the capability for successful coping identical or dissimilar to mental health.

In this chapter the emphasis is on coping *with everyday stress* and its relationship to mental health. One way of understanding mental health is as a complex, stable characteristic for describing psychological well-being and the realistic and adequate functioning of the individual. Whether such a construct eventually becomes superfluous when it can be defined through more behaviorally relevant correlates (for example, coping with stress) must be left undecided for the moment.

Others before us, such as Platt and Spivack (1974), Ilfeld (1980), Becker (1984a), and Fisher (1986), have also tried to draw an explicit connection between mental health and coping behavior. Platt and Spivack defined criteria for mental health on the basis of not being a psychiatric patient; Ilfeld through psychiatric and psychological characteristics such as symptoms, judgement of self-efficacy, etc.. Becker used a scale he developed which had proved to be a stable construct and was based on components such as social adaptability, emotional stability, self-fulfillment, and intelligence (Becker, 1984b). All of the above used questionnaires to record stress and coping behavior. The results of these studies show that the adequacy of the different types of coping behavior cannot be judged independently of the characteristics of the stressful situation (see chapter 1). There are, nevertheless, some general tendencies: Less mentally healthy persons resign more easily in problematic situations, they are not as able to accept uncontrollable stressors and thus are not as capable of re-evaluating, they show a higher tendency toward escape as well as a higher tendency toward self-blaming and aggression.

However, these rather situation-independent tendencies may be due more to tendencies toward generalizing in self-judgments (something Mischel (1968) found typical for self-report questionnaire data) than to overall nonspecific tendencies in the behavior. Real life data based on self-assessment taken near the time of the events are rarely available. The present study tests whether the expected situation-unspecific correlations appear even when the assessment of real coping behavior in everyday situations collected near the event are used. In this manner, evidence may be gathered to ascertain whether situation-independent criteria of adequacy for stress and coping can form the basis of criteria for mental health.

Hypotheses

The following hypotheses were studied:

(1) *Appraisals* of the situation: Mental health should be negatively correlated to the perceived valence, negatively correlated to the probability of the stressful events recurring, and positively correlated to the perceived controllability.

(2) *Emotional reactions* in the presence of stressors: Positive correlations should occur between the intensity of negative affect and negative indicators of mental health.

(3) *Coping behavior:* In mentally unhealthy persons there should be more dysfunctional reactions detrimental to well-being, both with respect to the self and the environment. For example, more self-blaming, less re-evaluation and active problem solving, more passivity and evasion should be correlated with negative indicators of mental health. Efficiency of coping behavior: Solving the problem should be positively correlated with mental health and discrepancies between ideal and real coping behavior should be negatively correlated with mental health. For the distinction of 'efficiency' and 'efficacy', see chapter 11, first part).

Method

The subjects practised the computer-assisted self-observation method using the COMRES system described in chapter 4. The procedure made possible (1) the direct compilation of experiential and behavioral data with a minimum of distortions due to the latency period between the event and the assessment thereof, as well as (2) the structured recording of psychologically relevant data. The program poses a series of stressor-related questions, which the user answers by entering the data related to his experiences and observations. The method records information - as described in chapter 4 - on the subject's perception of the situation (e.g., controllability of the stressor), his emotional reactions in the light of the stressor, his self- and environment-directed attempts at coping with the situation, the effectiveness of coping behavior, causal attributions, and the representativeness of his behavior.

The subject first learns to use the self-observation system via a user's manual (cf. Reicherts, Perrez & Matathia, 1986), and is given the general instructions. The subject is also requested to record at least 30 episodes.

As indicators of mental health we used Becker's (1984b) SDSG Scale, which consists of six bipolar self-rating scales that seek information on situation-independent, general personality characteristics such as 'nervous vs. calm' or 'uncertain vs. self-confident'. Becker reports an internal consistency of the scale of .77. In addition, we used the Purpose in Life Test (PIL) in the form as translated and revised by Becker (1984) (cf. Crumbaugh & Maholick, 1972, 1981), the internal consistency of which is, according to Becker, .91. Additional indicators utilised were the Beck's Depression Inventory (BDI; Beck et al., 1986) and Spielberger's State-Trait-Anxiety Inventory (STAI) by Laux et al. (1981).

Sample and procedure

The subjects of this study were part of the COMRES sample reported in chapter 4 (not all instruments were administered to the whole sample). The sub-sample consisted of N=40 adults (19 males and 21 females; mean age 26.8 years; 27 singles). All persons taking part in the experiment were university students, 40% of them were students of psychology.

When asked about somatic symptoms, 72.5% of the subjects reported having no problems or diseases, and 20% minor problems or diseases, the remaining subjects (7.5%) having major problems or diseases. In relation to current mental stress, 47.5% reported no stress, 40% minor stress, and 12.5% major stress. Thus, we are dealing here with a typical student population. The subjects were recruited from the universities of Fribourg and Bern (Switzerland) and received SFr. 50.-for their participation. Data collection started with completion of the questionnaires, and after a period of training the self-observation period using the COMRES, which took 4 to 5 weeks. Data collection was concluded with a debriefing.

Results

Distribution of stressors according to theme and content

Table 19. Classification of the recorded stressful episodes by students

number of episodes recorded	N = 1457
classification according to type of stressor	%
loss	14.8
harm	17.0
threat	32.6
challenge	35.6
classification according to domain of life	%
intrapsychic events	12.9
somatic events	6.7
studies, stages, job	21.8
social relations	38.4
- students, professors, colleagues	5.1
- family, relatives	3.7
- partner, close friends	14.8
- friends	11.3
- strangers	3.5
daily life activities	10.0
leisure	3.2
apartment	2.9
institutions	1.4
social and political events	0.7
study itself	1.7

An average of 36.4 stress episodes was recorded by each of the subjects, with a range from 29 to 60. About 80% of all recorded episodes were initial episodes, i.e. were not connected to previous episodes.

For the correlations, the mean values per variable and person of all initial episodes were used as appraisal and coping characteristics. The mean number of initial episodes per person was 29.

The recorded stress situations were printed out after the observation phase and presented to the subjects during the post interview; they were then asked to attach the situations to a predetermined content-analytic system with respect to a number of different characteristics. First, they had to assign stress situations to the categories 'loss, injury, threat or challenge'; then they assigned them according to an additional set of characteristics. This subjective assignment resulted in the categories listed in table 19.

The distribution of the stressors according to the content analysis reveals that in our sample problems with social relationship are in a higher rank than difficulties with study, and that the cognitive evaluations of the stressors as challenge or as threat are approximately equal.

Coping with stress and mental health

Table 20 shows the product-moment correlations between the coping variables and the above-mentioned indications of mental health (the polarity of the SDSG scales was reversed).

The correlations of the COMRES values with indicators of mental health uphold the hypotheses to varying degrees. The SDSG and PIL indicators of mental health correlate with the perception of valence with respect to *situation appraisal*. The better mental well-being is, and the better the subject's sense of meaning in life, the less stressors are felt to actually be a burden. The person's perception of controllability, on the other hand, does not correlate, as was expected, with these indicators of mental health. Also, the expected probability of the stressors recurring is negatively correlated with mental health (SDSG). Findings using the BDI and the anxiety variables are similar.

The extent of *emotional reaction* when faced with the recorded stressful situations proved to be significant on the dimensions 'nervous-calm', 'depressed-cheerful', 'angry-gentle', 'hesitant-spontaneous', 'lethargic-energetic', and 'abandoned-cared for' in 20 of the possible 30 correlations.

For *self-directed coping* behavior, mental health (as measured by SDSG and PIL) proved to be negatively correlated to the tendency to self- and other-blaming, and positively correlated to the ability to re-evaluate the stressful situation. The tendency for self-blaming also correlated with the BDI and anxiety indicators. Suppression of information suppression is correlated with depression.

Table 20. Correlations between stress and coping in episodes of daily life (COMRES self-observation) and psychological health indicators: depression (BDI), state- and trait-anxiety (STAI-S and STAI-T), mental health (SDSG) and positive perspectives in life (PIL)

	BDI	STAI-S	STAI-T	SDSG	PIL
appraisals of situation:					
ambiguity					
negative valence	.46[c]	.44[c]	.41[c]	.51[d]	-.38[b]
controllability					
changeability		-.31[b]			
probability of reoccurrence	.41[c]	.27[a]		-.37[b]	-.27[a]
familiarity	.32[b]			-.40[c]	-.27[a]
emotional reactions:					
anxious/nervous		.34[b]	.32[b]	-.48[c]	
depressed	.45[c]	.46[c]	.42[c]	-.41[c]	-.32[b]
aggressive	.31[b]	.34[b]			
hesitant		.39[b]	-.28[a]	-.34[b]	
lethargic			.28[a]	.27[a]	
abandoned	.52[d]	.40[c]	.53[d]	-.51[d]	-.44[c]
self-directed coping behavior:					
suppression of information	.36[c]				
search of information					
re-evaluation			-.35[b]	.38[b]	.27[a]
palliation					
self-blaming	.47[c]	.32[b]	.39[b]	-.43[c]	-.42[c]
other-blaming				-.39[b]	
environment-directed coping behavior:					
active influence on stressor					
evasion (escape, avoidance)	.49[c]				
passivity (hesitating, waiting)	.37[b]		.32[b]		
help from others					
coping efficiency:					
problem solving	-.29[a]	-.34[a]		.35[b]	
discrepancy ideal/real behavior	.33[b]	.48[c]	.49[c]	-.56[d]	

a p<.10; b p<.05; c b<.01; d p<.001;

Concerning *environment-directed* coping tendencies, it had been predicted that mentally healthy persons would show less passivity and evasion and more situation-oriented activity. Yet only on the BDI did we find the expected results with respect to evasion and passivity.

Clearer results were found in the *efficiency* of the practiced coping behavior. The expected correlations with the actual effectiveness of one's own coping behavior (goal attainment) were exhibited both with respect to the affective well-being (SDSG) and with depression and state anxiety (STAI). Also the discrepancy between actual coping behavior and ideal coping behavior is associated in the predicted direction in four of the five possible correlations.

Discussion

In this study, correlations were found between the various indicators of mental health and characteristics of the ability to cope with stress in real everyday situations. The overall picture is one of meaningful relationships. When individual indicators are studied more closely, the connections become even clearer.

The indicators of mental health (SDSG and PIL) correlate with the perception of valence of everyday stressors. SDSG is associated with goal attainment, the subjective (or perceived) effectiveness of one's coping. This is consistent with the view of Lazarus and Folkman (1984, 1987), who were of the opinion that everyday stress is experienced, by persons competent in coping with stress, as less harmful and is overcome by them in a more problem-focused manner. A relatively consistent pattern may also be seen in the tendency toward depression as measured by the BDI. For example, the higher subjects score on the BDI, the more the recorded everyday situations are judged as stressful and the more probable they expect the reoccurrence of the stressor to be. In addition their emotional reactions, when faced with stressors, are stronger. They seek out more information, express more self- and other-blaming during stressful situations, and are less ready to re-evaluate stressors. They also show more passivity and evasion in their reactions toward the environment. Higher depression values also correlate with the discrepancy between real and ideal coping with stress capabilities.

In general this is a parsimonious picture of depression and coping based on a new set of data resulting not from a retrospective point of view, or from questionnaires on hypothetical situations, but from structured descriptions of real life stress episodes, with only short latency times between their beginning and being recorded. The fact that mental health is operationalized for the most part through indicators of emotionality does not trivialize the connections to the COMRES variables; these are not based solely on emotional status, but also on cognitive and coping actions. They don't refer primarily to global traits but concern real life situations. In this sense, COMRES has proved effective as a field method of data collection. As to the connections between coping with stress and trait-anxiety, our findings confirm those of Houston (1982) who discovered that persons with higher trait-anxiety correlations tended to intellectualize less and not to plan any coping strategy. In our study, we discovered correlations with analog variables, i.e., with a deficit in re-evaluation, with increased self-blaming, and with an increased discrepancy between realized and desired behavior as well as with passivity. It should also be noted that the correlations between the STAI-state and the STAI-trait values and coping with stress differ only marginally.

Like the questionnaire studies on the correlations between mental health and coping behavior, this study, based on coping data collected in the field and near the event, confirms in part the idea that mentally healthy persons may be characterized via certain general characteristics in their way of dealing with everyday stress. A confounding of the variables of coping with those of mental health, as may be suspected in many well-known studies (Lazarus, De Longis, Folkman & Gruen, 1985), can be excluded here in the light of the data sources used. The results allow the interpretation that the more or less stable indicators of mental health are long-term effects of short-term behavior outcomes, i.e. of coping behaviors. The distinctive point for the short-term outcomes is the question of whether the individual disposes of tendencies to cope in an efficient manner with real life stressful episodes (cf. Becker, 1991).

On the other hand, when analyzing our findings one should take into account that there were no correlations in a number of cases. Our method is in need of further differentiation. Future studies should concentrate on an analysis of coping behavior with respect to the psychologically relevant situational characteristics. Using the COMRES methodology it is clear that it is not the adaptation to objective features of situations which can be studied, but rather the emotional, cognitive and behavioral response pattern as a reaction to the perception of situational characteristics. We can analyze adaptation processes to subjective perceptions of stressful situations (see chapter 1), as assessed by our recording system. This analysis makes it possible to study the relative adaptational value of different coping responses as a function of certain subjectively perceived features of stressful situations. Within the intra-personal reference system the statement of Krohne makes sense in that 'the degree of efficiency of a strategy (is) a function of specific (sub-jective) situational characteristics' (Krohne, 1986). Situation-independent statements concerning criteria of adequate coping behavior will be limi-ted. *The question then is not whether mentally healthy persons show less passivity and evasion and more active coping behavior when faced with stressors, but rather whether they tend to act in this manner when faced with subjectively controllable stressors.* With uncontrollable stressors we would expect perhaps evasion, passivity, re-evaluation, etc. A new metho-dology to study the efficiency of coping behavior taking into account subjective situational features is presented in chapter 11 which describes the behavior-rule approach.

10. Work stress in medical care units

Meinrad Perrez, Robert Matathia, Roberto Malacrida, Daria Bomio and Michael Reicherts

Introduction

The computer-assisted recording system of coping with stress (COMRES) episodes in everyday life - as described previously (see chapter 4) was developed for the observation and measurement of stress and coping by individuals. Another type of question arises if the 'stress of an institution' is to be analysed. It is clear that institutions cannot experience stressful encounters. Psychological stress is a privilege of higher organisms. Nevertheless, institutions or working units can be described in terms of their stress inducing characteristics and can be analysed in their typical qualities of stress inducing elements. Four important classes of factors constitute the sources of possible stress in institutions (e.g. McGrath, 1976): administration and social rules of functioning, work demands (tasks), physical features of the working environment and features of the social environment. From a psychological point of view these factors - intervening in real life stressful situations to a varying degree - can be examined with regard to controllability, changeability, valence, probability of reoccurrence etc. In the present chapter we try to work out a taxonomy of stressful situations on the basis of these situation variables. Furthermore, we analyse, among other things, the connection between types of situation and coping features.

In order to get a psychological picture of the stress profile of a working unit, the problem of accessing psychologically relevant field data has to be dealt with. Until now the recording of psychological data on stress and coping behavior *in caring professionals*, as in other working professions, has been concentrated on questionnaire and interview data (Gray-Toft & Anderson, 1981; Robinson & Lewis, 1989). A special type of questionnaire, not referring to experienced stressful episodes, but to hypothetical situations, asks people to react to imagined situations

(Jacobson, 1983). In some studies authors used participant observation (e.g. Coombs & Goldman, 1973).

A version of the COMRES which could be installed on a PC was developed in order to observe stress and coping in a medical care unit. One of the purposes of the study was to evaluate the new method of measurement of stress in working units, and to assess its practicability. A second aim of the study - beyond a phenomenological description of stressors and their frequencies - was to determine an empirically guided classification of stressors in this unit. Thirdly, we intended to analyse the connection of types of situations, elaborated by correspondence analysis, with coping features. Finally, some relations between characteristics of care staff - like professional experience or level of professional education - and stress experience were analysed, using questionnaire data.

Method

Assessment of stress and coping

The programme COMRES, originally conceived for pocket computers (SHARP PC-1360; see chapter 4), was adapted for the DOS operating system for Personal Computers. Programmed in BASIC, it stores the subjects' data in sequential ASCII files. This version of COMRES is multi-user, in the sense that different people may successively enter their stressful episodes. Each user is identified by an individual code, which he or she chooses. The programme manages the files so that the same code cannot designate two different individuals.

The PC represents an *external memory* of stress experienced while working in the care unit. Its use allows participants, applying their private code, to store the psychologically relevant information just after the stressful experience in the care unit. They are asked - with few exceptions - for the same information with the same response formats as in the original COMRES version. The participants were introduced to the self-observation system and trained how to operate the system, which is easy to master.

For further data the Nursing Stress Scale (NSS) of Gray-Toft and Anderson (1981) and a questionnaire about socio-demographic and professional information were administered. The NSS is a questionnaire asking for frequencies of typical stressful medical care situations. The total score is obtained by the addition of the values of the 7 subscales.

The *independent variables* are: different *care units*, distinguishing general care units, intensive care unit (ICU) and urgent care unit (UCU). The variable *level of professional training* of the nurses was divided in three degrees: 'without professional training' (unskilled people), 'in training' and 'with accomplished professional training'. *Professional experience* was operationalized by the number of years that the nurses had worked in this professional field. We formed three groups: less than 5 years, from 5 to 10 years, and more than 10 years.

Sample

The computer-aided self-observation method was used by staff members of an intensive care unit (ICU) and an urgent care unit (UCU). Out of 31 nurses invited to take part, 16 actually did so. During a period of 12 weeks 186 stressful events (mean per person n = 11.5) were entered and stored on the PC. All the nurses in the hospital were invited to participate in the questionnaire study by answering the Nursing Stress Scale. 49 accepted the invitation (see table 21).

Table 21. Sample of the medical care study; number of responders (non-responders)

	Nursing Stress Scale NSS	Computer-aided self observation COMRES
general medical unit	18	- -
intensive care unit ICU	18	13 (5)
urgent care unit UCU	13	3 (10)
total	49	16 (15)

Results

Distribution and taxonomy of stressors stored by the COMRES-PC

The stressful episodes the nurses stored on the COMRES-PC system are illustrated by the following *examples*:

'I am working this morning with a colleague who's style of interaction with the patient annoys me. It disturbs me to see how she is treating adult patients like children.'

'A very old patient just died. No clear decision was made during several hours. I'm uptight; I'm not sure if it's because the doctor was so hesitant or because the patient was in so much pain.'

'Although I informed the physician on the deterioration of the patient's health status, he did not take my therapeutic suggestions into consideration.'

Content analysis of the 186 stressful episodes stored by the 16 staff members who took part in the study gives the following picture (see table 22). A psychology student and a nurse were trained to apply the categorial schemata. They independently analysed the episodes of the sample and allocated them to the relevant categories; a few episodes which did not fit clearly were discussed by the two raters.

Table 22: Classification of the recorded COMRES episodes (N=186)

categories of nursing stress scale (NSS)	scale no.	% of episodes	stressor domains	% of episodes
death and dying	1	33.1%	patient and family	39.3%
work load	6	32.1%	administration	36.2%
others	-	10.2%	interpersonal relations	17.6%
conflict with physicians	2	8.6%	others	4.8%
conflict with other nurses	5	8.6%	psychological environment	2.1%
uncertainty conc. treatment	7	4.8%		
inadequate preparation	3	2.1%		100.0%
lack of support	4	0.5%		
		100.0%		

For the first content analysis the subscales of the NSS (e.g. 'work load' or 'death and dying') were used as categories (see table 22, left side). The relative frequencies of the different types of stressful events show a conspicuous amount in the categories 'death and dying' (about 33%) and 'work load' (about 32%). Stressful situations were attributed to the category 'work load', if the described problem resulted from properties of the special nursing task the subject had to execute, for example assistance in medical interventions demanding a high technical competence.

Another classification (see table 22, right side) of the recorded 186 stressful events reveals about 38% of the episodes as 'problems with patients and their families', 34.2% as 'problems with the administration' of the ICU and UCU, and 19.4% as 'problems concerning interpersonal relations'.

Taxonomy of stressful situations

In order to describe the totality of the data and to work out a taxonomy of situations by analysing their relationships, we used correspondence analysis (factor analysis of multiple correspondences) treating the set of situations as individuals, and the features of the situations as active variables.

Figure 9. Situation characteristics of two types of stressful episodes in medical care

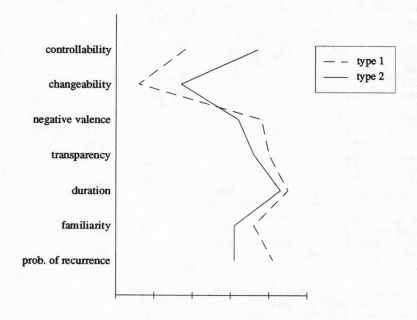

A hierarchical clustering analysis was then performed by aggregating - according to Ward's criterion - the set of situations characterized by

their principle coordinates. A partition was constructed by truncation of the hierarchical tree, which has been characterized by a description procedure. The analyses were conducted using the program SPAD.N (Lebart, Morineau & Lambert, 1987) on a DEC microVAX computer.

Table 23. COMRES variables in the 2 types of nursing stress episodes (N=186 episodes)

	situation class		t-test[1]
	1 (n=68)	2 (n=118)	
perceived situation characteristics:			
controllability	1.79	3.67	[2]
changeability	0.62	1.70	
negative valence	3.84	3.15	
ambiguity	4.04	3.61	
probability of reoccurrence	4.09	3.09	
familiarity	3.56	3.09	
duration	4.49	4.27	
emotional reactions*:			
anxious/nervous	1.62	1.90	-1.41[a]
depressed	1.69	2.26	-2.89[c]
aggressive	1.31	1.82	-2.76[c]
hesitant	2.62	3.02	-1.88[b]
lethargic	2.71	3.12	-1.83[a]
abandoned	2.00	2.56	-2.57[c]
environment-directed coping:			
active influence	1.15	1.35	-1.76[b]
passivity (hesitate, wait)	0.63	0.47	1.62[a]
evasion (escape, avoid)	0.43	0.30	1.38[a]
self-directed coping behavior:			
re-evaluation	0.78	1.06	-2.57[c]
palliation	1.00	0.85	1.37[a]
other-blaming	0.90	0.54	2.81[c]
coping efficiency:			
problem solving	1.68	1.85	-1.60[a]
discrepancy ideal/real beh.	1.52	1.32	1.90[b]
attribution of outcome:			
internal	0.34	0.51	-1.49[a]
external (persons)	1.29	0.90	2.19[b]
external (circumstances)	2.15	1.79	2.15[b]

* high values indicate low intensities of emotion; [1] one-tailed; [2] appraised situation characteristics were active clustering variables; all differences are significant (p<.05)
[a] p<.10; [b] p<.05; [c] p<.01; [d] p<.001

The first axis obtained by the correspondance analysis puts the two types of situation in opposition:

(1) The situations of cluster 1 (n=68) have a strong negative valence, they are less controllable and changeable and ambiguous than the other class. Furthermore, they last about one day or more, and they are rather recurrent and familiar. This 'depression-inducing' cluster reveals a high similarity to the situations of type 2 described in chapter 4, except the variable 'transparency'.

(2) The other situations (n=118) are attached to cluster 2. These situations are less stressful, more controllable and more changeable than situations of the first cluster. They are also less recurrent and less familiar. The configuration of their characteristics is in some respects similar to type 3 situations described in chapter 4.

Analysis of variance reveals a strong multivariate effect of the cluster partition ($F_{(1,184)}=359.81$; $p<.001$). Figure 6 depicts the configurations of the situation characteristics (centroids) of the two clusters of stressful situations recorded by the nurses.

Types of situations and stress and coping behavior

Table 23 also shows the mean levels of some stress and coping variables for the two clusters of situations and their statistically significant differences. Concerning *emotional reactions*, the results reveal that the (more stressful) class 1 situations are more than class 2 situations associated with feelings of depression, anger, abandonment, low spontaneity, and low vigour. *Coping behavior* is oriented more towards blaming others, and less to re-evaluating one's own situation or to influencing the stressor in an active way. Instead there is a trend to more evasive and passive coping behavior. *Causal attributions* of the outcome are more external, i.e. on other persons and circumstances, and the difference between real and ideal coping after the subjects' appraisal is higher in this type of situations than in the less stressful type 2 situations. Also coping efficiency is lower.

Relations between care staff and NSS-stress

Different characteristics of care staff were analysed to examine their association with stress. In the first comparison nurses *working full time*

(N=35) were compared with nurses *working part time* (N=14) using analysis of variance. A multivariate analysis of variance with the seven categories of the NSS as dependent variables revealed a significant difference ($F_{(7,41)}$; p=.02) between groups. Nurses working part time reported more stress, especially concerning conflict with physicians and uncertainty about treatment.

If *professional training* is considered as an independent variable - the distinction being 'without professional training' (N=18), 'in training' (N=8), and 'with accomplished training' (N=23) - we find by univariate tests for significance that the group 'in training' describes the highest stress (helplessness) in situations, where patients fail to improve and in situations with uncertainty regarding the operation and the functioning of specialized equipment.

As third independent variable - *professional experience* - distinguished three groups of nurses:
(i) under 5 years (N=15), (ii) from 5 to 10 years (N=17), and (iii) over 10 years (N=15) experience (the relevant information was missing from one subject). A univariate test of the frequencies of stressors experienced between the 3 groups indicates higher values for the group with the lowest extent of experience, and the lowest values for the group with the highest extent of experience for the NSS-categories 'death and dying' and 'uncertainty about treatment'.

Comparing the NSS-data of the different *care units*, there are differences in the frequency of stressors between the units. A univariate test indicates that the items explaining the differences are items concerning death and patients' dying, and workload ($F_{(3,44)}$=3.8; p=.03). Nurses from the *general medical units* (N=18) and the ICU (N=18) suffer more from these stressors than the nurses from the UCU (N=13).

Discussion

The computer-aided self-observation system produced interesting information on real life problems in two care units in a hospital. About half of the invited staff members took part in the aspect of the study which utilised the COMRES-PC method. They stored 186 stressful episodes over a period of 12 weeks. These stored episodes allow a stress diagnosis to be made of the institution. The observation-data were completed by questionnaire data.

The findings underline, on a *descriptive and phenomenological level*, the particular importance of four categories of *stressful episodes reported by the nurses* of the ICU and UCU: problems concerning death and patients' dying, problems in the context of work load, problems related to administration and problems with other nurses. 'Death and dying' and 'work load' are also the two most frequent problems described by the whole sample (N=49) in the NSS questionnaire (not mentioned above). There is a certain convergence of results stemming from the NSS questionnaire and the COMRES assessment system.

Problems inherent to the tasks of the medical care system could be separated from *problems the system has with itself.* The first type of problem is more or less natural, resulting from the purpose of medical care. Hospitals were invented to aid and support patients and their relatives; and death and dying or problems with work load, to some extent, are characteristic problems of this profession. However, problems with administration, with other nurses or with physicians are problems of the system itself. They hinder the institution in its original function. They must be the first object of intervention in order to improve the functioning of care units. Gachowetz (1988) found in his study similar results and analysed the role of the organizational climate more precisely.

Using correspondence analysis, it was possible to find two different types of situations reported by the COMRES-PC; namely situations with a longer temporal extension, with low changeability and high controllability, with a high probability of reoccurrence (type 2), and situations with a high negative valence, low ambiguity and low controllability (type 1). The first type of situation is more related to negative, stressful emotions and to coping behavior which consists of blaming others and which shows little tendency to re-evaluate and to confront the stressor in an active manner. The results show the impact of situation on behavior. This cluster of situations seems to represent situations which induce emotions of helplessness (depressive, aggressive, abandoned, etc.) and coping responses. It is to be supposed that the subjects in our small sample were not depressed people in a pathological sense at all. But even among normal people this kind of situation increases the probability of a pattern of behavior which has some similarities with depressive behavior.

The results show that the encounter with stressful events in a hospital is not independent from professional training and experience. Keane, Ducette and Adler (1985) found similar connections. In contrast to Landeweerd and Boumans (1988) we could not find higher levels of

NSS-stress in the ICU and UCU. For several items general medical units produced higher levels of stress, for example the item 'death and patients' dying', which can be explained by a closer personal relationship with the patients, who stay longer on the unit than in ICU and UCU (cf. Harris, Bond & Turnbull, 1990).

It is not totally clear to what extent the results are representative especially concerning the results obtained using the COMRES-PC method. Not all members of the unit participated in the study. Imagine, for example, if the non-participants were the 'sources' of the interpersonal problems reported! There is not only the potential for bias in the participant's selection of specific situations, but also from the process of self-selection (with possible interactions between personal characteristics, motivation to participate, and stress perception and coping). In principle, it is possible to prevent these problems. It would be desirable therefore to know more about the motivations of the staff who took part. With reference to the number of nurses willing to take part in the study, the results are certainly more representative for the ICU than for the UCU. One reason for the high non-participation rate in the UCU may be the fact that the COMRES-PC was placed in the neighbouring ICU, and therefore more inaccessible for UCU staff.

In conclusion we think that the proposed method can be considered as a first step. If the results refer to the majority of the members of a (sub)system and if there are a certain number of episodes reported, the results of stress analysis can help to prepare for organizational changes, e.g. organizational development, changes in the time schedule etc. In addition, the results can help to prepare training programs to improve coping behavior. Well founded typologies of stressful episodes, similar to the proposed dimensional taxonomy, are an interesting instrument for all organizational diagnostics.

Case studies IV: Do empirical findings from group studies improve one's understanding of the individual?

This section demonstrates how to use results from empirical research using SCPQ and COMRES data for individual case analysis.

The empirical results of validation studies support different types of statistically founded conclusions, namely:

(1) The ascription of characteristics to the person on the basis of specific aspects of his or her stress and coping behavior.

(1.1) Classification of a person in a diagnostic class, such as a clinical syndrome, e.g. the ascription of the DSM-III diagnosis 'major depression'.

(1.2) Assigning the person a quantitative characteristic, such as the amount of depression (e.g. in terms of BDI) or the value(s) of a more complex indicator, such as psycological health (including several facets by different measures: 'positive self-concept', 'absence of psycho-somatic symptoms', 'satisfying social relations', 'high professional adaptation' etc.).

(2) The prediction of future characteristics or events on the basis of diagnostic features previously assessed:

(2.1) Assigning of a class variable (e.g. higher mortality risk related to coronary diseases, when coping over a long time with a type-A behavior pattern).

(2.2) Assigning a quantitative variable as positive self-concept or positive life perspective ('a positive perspective of professional life after losing a job').

The validation results of stress and coping behavior measured by the COMRES self-assessment system or by the SCPQ questionnaire presented here only allow ascriptions (except the prediction in chapter ...). The comparison between depressed and nondepressed groups can reveal a *pattern* of stress and coping behavior which is *specific to depression* and which is different to the behavior of nondepressed 'normal' control subjects. Neither Harry nor Evelyn seems to belong to the depressed pattern.

It is possible to use so called *discriminant functions* to assign the person to a syndrome or a class - e.g. 'depression' - using a statistical procedure. This type of analysis is described in chapter 7. When taking the SCPQ test values for Evelyn and transforming them into the discriminant function of the depression study, she clearly belongs to the class of non-depressed 'normal' people. Her pattern of situation appraisal, her emotional behavior, and her coping efforts differ in nearly all aspects from the depressed pattern. The decision to discriminate between diagnostic classes is based on statistical parameters, i.e. a decision made under conditions described by probabilities and not by certainty. Therefore we need an indicator of the quality of such a multivariate assignment to classes; one indicator is the ratio of right vs. wrong predictions achieved by the use of this discriminant function. In the study of depressed vs. non-depressed control subjects, referring to all SCPQ variables and all episodes, the assignment was 100% correct. It represents a high probability of making a correct diagnosis of depression taking into account the proposed characteristics of stress and coping.

Imagine a depressed woman in Evelyn's situation: she would perhaps spend a lot of time looking for the earring. Unable to accept the loss she would then despair and would continue to feel sad for an excessively long time. Transforming her responses in the SCPQ process questionnaire into the discriminant function will show her to be in the depressed class.

Correlation measures between COMRES or SCPQ diagnosis and indicators such as psychic health help us to understand other aspects of a person in facilitating the ascription of other properties. Given the association of COMRES coping with *self-blaming* and reduced *psychic health* (e.g. trait anxiety $r=.39$; depression $r=.47$; positive self-concept $r=-.43$; see chapter 9), a person with a strong self-blame coping tendency can be predicted to have lower psychic health (multiple correlation $r=-.57$). Here too, prediction is not deterministic, but statistic, referring to the strength of correlation and the similarity to the reference population. For example, knowing the self-blaming tendency of a person as high vs. low (over vs. under the median of a reference population) helps us to ascribe psychic health as high or low with a certain probability of being right (70%), which is at least some 40% better than chance (see also chapter 5).

If we refer to the *situational aspect* of our two protagonists' coping tendencies, taking into account the results described in case studies III, other characteristics, which were not considered above, can be fictionally illustrated. Suppose Harry and Evelyn did report several self-observations of their coping behavior in two types of situations (aversive vs. loss), - or having the questionnaire-data at our disposal -, their tendencies concerning 'suppression of information' may be as follows (see figure 10). The pattern may also be true for their tendencies assessed using the SCPQ questionnaire data. The figure depicts differences between personal coping tendencies (Harry suppresses more information) as well as differences between types of stressful situations (there is more suppression of information in situations of loss).

Figure 10: Suppression of information as situation and person specific coping tendency

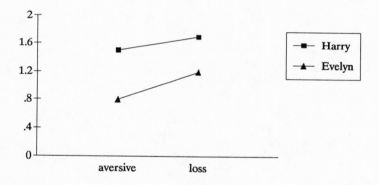

GRIMSBY INSTITUTE OF

LIBRARIES

FURTHER & HIGHER EDUCATION

11. Adequate coping behavior: The behavior rules approach

Michael Reicherts and Meinrad Perez

Effective, efficient, and adequate coping with stress

The question of what is meant by *adequate coping* has been discussed repeatedly in the past years. Vaillant (1976) and Andrews, Tennant, Hewson, and Schonell (1978) tried to define the adequacy of coping styles by referring to 'maturity'. According to Vaillant (1976), 'immature' styles, for example, would be acting out and denial, which in normal development are successively replaced by more 'mature' styles such as sublimation, altruism, delay of reinforcement, and so on. Antonovsky (1979) delineated three criteria for mature behavior: rationality, flexibility, and farsightedness. These authors have attempted to lend support to their theories by correlating maturity scores with scores for mental well-being.

Lazarus (Lazarus, 1983; Lazarus & Folkman, 1984) discussed criteria of adequacy under two aspects: (a) the time dimension 'short- vs. long-term- effects', (b) the various dimensions of effects, depending on one's contentment with social relations on the one hand, and on one's personal well-being or physical health on the other. Yet homogeneity of effect cannot be assumed a priori with respect to either the time or the effect dimensions: short-term positive effects on one dimension may prove to be negative on another, or in the long run.

Characterizing the ability to successfully cope with stress as a process of successful adaptation to internal or external stressors (White, 1974) is circular reasoning because the nature of successful coping and adaptation remains unaddressed. The latter can be defined more precisely in terms of attaining a particular goal: for example, affect control, if the stressor is primarily of an affective, system-internal type; or external problem solving, if the stressor is primarily of system-external nature. Thus, adequacy is defined on the basis of effect. Silber et al. (1961), Krohne (1984), and Schönpflug (1985) further 'complicate' the matter by relating the effectiveness to the costs. Krohne differentiates between 'effectiveness' and 'efficiency', the former describing performance, the latter the physical energy required for the performance. Schönpflug and Battmann (1988) distinguish between structural and energetic, internal and external resources invested in coping with stressful situations. They show that the emotional costs can have a disproportionate relationship to the benefit gained on the level of system-external problem solving (e.g. type-A behavior) and therefore have to be 'managed' in stressful episodes.

The reconstruction of adequate coping behavior

A *performed, single behavior* is effective when it leads to the desired goal of the purposeful act or the purposive behavior. A *type or class of behavior* can be characterized - independently of its performance - in terms of probabilities for effectiveness. It is deemed *adequate* when it - independently of the effectiveness in any one single case - corresponds to several criteria of rationality, including among others the cost-benefit relationship. We assume here that adequate acts are acts referring to behavior types with high probabilities for effectiveness since one criterium of rationality lies in the empirical reliability of the behavior type as means to reach a particular goal (Patry & Perez, 1982). For a circumscribed domain we formulated rules for adequate coping which refer to the psychologically relevant characteristics of the stressor.

We can now define several relevant terms more precisely: *effectiveness* (or efficacy) of coping can be defined as the variable characterizing the extent of goal attainment, i.e. the extent of stress reduction. This variable concerns the attained adaptation level without considering costs such as (physical and psychic) effort, spent time, and so on. *Efficiency* represents a more complex feature of coping, relating criteria of effectiveness and *cost*. It can be defined as the 'ratio of the number of problems solved to the effort invested in a task (e.g. time spent preparing for an exam or in controlling situations)' (Krohne, 1984), or as the degree of goal attainment (stress-reduction) in relation to the costs. Both, efficiency and effectiveness can characterize a concrete single coping behavior or process performed, and a type or class of coping behavior independent of its performance (e.g. as anticipated).

Adequacy or appropriateness of coping: the rule-approach

Adequacy or *appropriateness* of coping are evaluative terms. They describe ideal criteria for behavior, and a real life coping encounter or a coping style can be judged against these criteria. Is it possible to determine such criteria and to found them empirically?

As mentioned in the beginning, one way to define adequacy of behavior was to analyse its 'maturity'. Menaghan (1982) criticizes the maturity-approach by pointing out that it says nothing about real behavior in stressful situations. In addition, such general ideal or negative criteria (e.g. 'denial') do not do justice to the broad range of possible situations. Situations arise in which denial can play a very constructive role (Lazarus, 1983). Another attempt at determining criteria of adequacy was made in studies in which subjects were asked which methods would be helpful to them in certain stressful situations. Boss, McCubbin, and Lester (1979), for example, questioned women about successful coping strategies for marital stress situations. Here, however, the effectiveness of coping strategies has been confounded by subjective opinion as to their effectiveness.

We assume that the development of criteria for adequate coping behavior is possible, if the problem which requires to be solved is formulated in a more precise way, i.e. as a behavior task, whose solution can be given on an empirical basis. Instead of 'What is appropriate or mature behavior?' we ask 'What are the features of appropriate actions if a person intends to reach a particular goal under certain internal and external conditions?'. This question can be answered - at least for some types of tasks. E.g. 'What is to be done if a person wants to reduce stress, if the external stressor is characterized by high controllability in the short term and if the person is strongly emotionally excited?' The goal in this case is stress reduction; internal conditions are characterized by high emotionality and the external stressor by high controllability. The answer to this type of question is a behavior rule. A good answer must meet criteria of rationality.

We propose to define coping behavior as adequate or appropriate if it corresponds to several criteria of rationality, including effectiveness and the cost-benefit relationship.

As *criteria* we suggest that the person's coping with stress in a given situation corresponds to a behavior rule, that (1) recommends this type of behavior in such a situation, because it is proved to be effective under the given internal and external situation features. (2) The costs and negative side effects have to be countered acceptably by the benefits. (3) The means to achieve stress reduction must be ethically acceptable.

Types of rules and the relationship between rules and behavior

Behavior rules (BR) can be interpreted as hypothetical imperatives with a conditional-normative structure: 'If a situation has the characteristics c, and if goal g is to be reached within time t, then behavior b is recommended to achieve g.' The structure of such statements is based on the linking of situation characteristics with proposed behavior relating to a specified goal. We would presuppose stress reduction as a generalized goal for coping with stress.

BR can be considered under two different aspects: (1) as hypothetical imperatives - independent of the individual - containing suggestions for behavior toward specific goals in certain situation conditions, or (2) as psychological phenomena - i.e. as personal and private thoughts on desirable behavior in specific situations (instrumental beliefs). According to Popper and Eccles (1977) BR would be in the first interpretation members of world 3, in the second interpretation members of world 2.

The BR 'If a stressor is controllable and you wish to reduce stress, try to influence it!' can be subject to scientific investigation and criticism as a hypothetical imperative, which is valid on a *inter*individual level. We can ask a person if he thinks in the same way, or if he prefers other suggestions. In this case we are referring to BR as individual mental phenomena. It is possible to compare individual instrumental beliefs - or private BR - with the *inter*individual BR, and also to compare the person's actual behavior with both types of rules.

Rule-orientation therefore involves two aspects: Behavior *rule-directedness* and *rule-conformity*. It is possible that a person behaves in accord with a rationally founded interindividual BR without representing this rule cognitively. His behavior is then rule-conforming but not rule-directed. Rule-conforming behavior is a necessary condition for rule-directed behavior, but not a sufficient condition. If behavior is rule-directed, the person consciously and intentionally applies the rule, which may be a private or interindividual one.

Dysfunctional coping behavior may be constituted by rule-directed behavior based on an inadequate private BR, or by inadequate behavior deviating from an adequate BR, or by inadequate behavior in the absence of any private BR.

We formulated behavior rules for *adequate coping* referring to a limited number of situation features (Reicherts, Käslin & Perrez, 1984). These types of behavior tasks take into consideration chiefly situations with moderate to high rather than low controllability, situations with high rather than low changeability and situations with high rather than low ambiguity. The rules are proposed for some of the typical configurations of these situation features.

Foundation and assessment of BR's and rule-oriented behavior

Everyone has at their disposal a set of private behavior rules, acquired in their learning history. How are we to distinguish rationally and *intersubjectively* (objectively) founded BRs from private BRs only *intrasubjectively* based? The first criterion to be met is that of effectiveness. The assertion that a certain type of behavior is required for the mastery of a certain type of situation must be empirically confirmed. We may, in addition, analyse if persons using these rules in their everyday lives differ in a desirable way from persons not using them.

Assessment of rule-oriented behavior

One of the main problems for the analysis of technological rules of everyday behavior is a methodological one. There are two mutually dependent aspects to this problem. First, what kind of a psychological construct is a BR? Second, how can we link the application of BRs to observable variables; i.e. how do we observe situation-behavior units in the natural setting?

BR's are conditional-normative in structure. In the stress and coping domain, BRs correspond to *coping strategies* (e.g. Lazarus & Folkman, 1984) which take into account features of the situation. BR's are hypothetical imperatives for behavior which refer to situation conditions (objective or subjective). Their effects/outcomes are described by desirable states which may correspond to the person's intended goals. BRs reflect know how.

We may try to elaborate private BR's directly by asking the person for her rules of coping with stress. In respect of their formulation and/or their content he or she may finally reveal highly idiosyncratic rules. To differentiate the individual rules and make them more comprehensive and/or intersubjectively comparable, we may further introduce different antecedents (situations), different goals, operators (behaviors) and efficiency criteria. But this direct approach is costly and presents a difficult task for the subject. In addition, rules explicated in this way have to be proved or tested in real life settings by observation, bearing in mind the actual goals of the person.

Rule-conformity analysis

One possible method to test behavior conforming to intersubjective rules is a procedure we called behavior *rule conformity analysis* (Reicherts, 1988). BRs are first translated into two groups of variables consisting of (a) those concerning the situation and (b) those concerning the behavior (including goals). The rules then describe the recommended situation-behavior contingency, e.g. high ambiguity ought to be associated with high search for information. Both variables 'ambiguity' and 'search for information' can be observed (using COMRES method, for example).

Rules may differ in regard to their formulation. The simplest form of rule is that which specifies conditions and behaviors qualitatively (e.g. 'If situation X, do not do Y! - If realization of Z is your goal'). If the rules rely on ordinal or quantitative information, the main issue becomes the degree to which levels of conditions, intensities etc. of behaviors covary - as in a cook's recipe.

One of the main purposes of analyzing coping behavior is the *intra*individual analysis of relations between the appraisal of the situation and coping responses (or trials). Observed contingencies of appraisals of situations and subsequent coping responses can be compared with the recommended contingencies. Observing populations of normal individuals may show how many people conform to such a rule, to what extent they conform to it, and how effective this is.

When performing a within-subject analysis of rule-conforming behavior, many snags are encountered with the usual statistical procedures, even the descriptive ones. Correlation measures require variance and most correlation measures are focused on linearity. Furthermore, testing statistical hypotheses (e.g. significance of correlations) within the individual presupposes independence of observations. However, linearity does not count necessarily for the connection of appraised situation features and behavior strength - the two elements of the rules. In principle different rules can lie on different scale levels, e.g. categorial vs. ordinal, what renders their correlations not easy to compare. In addition, independence of observation required for testing statistical hypotheses is rarely given.

The BR conformity index: Concept and procedure

A method is proposed for analyzing rule-conforming regularities which is contingency based, easy to apply and which seems psychologically plausible. It is inspired by prediction analysis (Hildebrand et al., 1977), and the analysis of attributions (e.g. Kelley, 1972). First we formalize a behavior rule by translating it into a *contingency pattern* connecting at least two variables: an antecedent variable (situation feature) and a consequent variable (feature of behavior or action). More than two variables are possible - e.g. we may include certain goal characteristics, or additional variables relating to antecedent or consequent aspects. A rule, then, is represented by the valid cells of the contingency table, which are defined a priori. They do not depend on marginal distributions. This contingency pattern must cover all levels of antecedent and consequent variables included by the rule, i.e. it has to be exhaustive. Implicit or unspecified values or value areas have to be explicitly described.

It is possible to represent rules very different in structure. To illustrate this, a *contingency pattern* which derives from several 3x3 value rules is shown in figure 11. *A* stands for the situation antecedent variable and *C* for the behavioral consequent variable, the values of both variables being in ascending order (from 1 to 3, ordinal or quantitative).

Example (1) describes a linear ascending 'the-more-A-the-more-C!' rule, e.g. the more at stake, the more one should try to influence the stressor! Example (2) is the inversion of rule 1 (the more A, the less C!). A kind of a 'coming to a point' pattern best describes (3). The higher the antecedent value, the more the behavior is precisely defined; and the lower the antecedent value, the less determined the consequent behavior can be. For example, the more is at stake, the more your attention is focused on the stressor's properties, and the less is at stake, the more you are free to control your attention. Example (4) demonstrates another non-linear structure: behavior values are clearly circumscribed on low or high situation values, in the middle area they are free to vary. Example (5) shows an inverted U-form: Only the highest antecedent value determines one (exact) behavior value (not too much, not too little!); the lower antecedent values are followed by either low or high behavior values.

Figure 11. Different structures of behavior rules
(A antecedent situation characteristics; C behavioral consequences)

```
  3 . . .      . . x    x . .    . . x    x . .    . x .
A 2 . . .      . x .    . x .    . x x    x x x    x . x
  1 . . .      x . .    . . x    x x x    x . .    x . x
    1 2 3
    C           (1)      (2)      (3)      (4)      (5)
```

Rule contingency patterns have some *formal properties:*

(1) *Differentiation:* the number of antecedent and consequent values discriminated by the contingency table. The above 3x3-value examples are more differentiated than for example a 2x2-value pattern.
(2) *Specifity:* the proportion of antecedent values which have specific consequent values, i.e. where antecedent-consequent-relation is unequivocal. Example (1) is more specific than (4), which, in turn, is more specific than (5).
(3) *Precision:* The lower the number of valid cells covered by the rule, the higher the precision. Example (1) is more precise than (4) which is more precise than (3).

To determine the amount of observations which follow the rule, the number of observations which lie in the valid cells covered by the rule must be calculated and then contrasted with the total number of observations. This is the BR conformity index:

$$CON = \frac{\text{observations in valid cells}}{\text{total number of observations}}$$

Given the following rule as an example (figure 12; left part). Suppose we made the following observations of a subject (figure 12; right part).

Figure 12. Contingency pattern of a behavior rule and conformity index CON of a sample of situation-behavior episodes observed

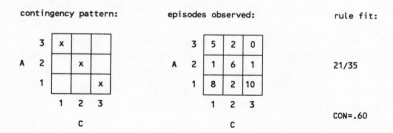

```
contingency pattern:        episodes observed:          rule fit:

    3  x                        3  5   2   0
A   2      x                 A  2  1   6   1              21/35
    1         x                 1  8   2   10

       1   2   3                   1   2   3
           c                           c                CON=.60
```

This case shows neither a very strong nor a very poor rule fit. The most deviant observations in terms of the rule are the observations of A1-C1 (n=8). These disturb the diagonal pattern of the matrix.

The value of the conformity index CON may vary according to the precision of the rule: the more valid cells, the greater the probability that observations are covered by the rule (assuming that they are equally probable). A simple measure of precision may be given by

$$P = \frac{\text{number of valid cells}}{\text{total number of cells}}$$

P can be understood as the percentage of observations that will be rule-conforming by chance, assuming the observations are equally distributed. When we are interested in comparing BR conformity within different contingency patterns, it would be helpful to relate each conformity value to the values which would be expected by chance:

$$CONp = CON/P$$

The proposed measure CON represents one approach to operationalize the degree of rule fit. It relies on *observed regularities* which should refer to theoretically founded features of situations and of behavior, which can be observed by the subject himself or by an observer in the natural or experimental setting (including data gathered by other methods).

In the following study, CON applies to rule conformity on the *'inner adjustment'* level, i.e. choice and control of behavior in relation to the subject's perception of the situation and of the outcome. Obviously the rule conformity analysis applies also to other types of correspondences as described in chapter 1 (e.g. objective features of situation, actual behavior and objective effects observed by independent and trained observers).

BR conformity indices are analysed as individual measures (based on the within-subject data pattern) and can be connected with other characteristics of the subject, e.g. trait anxiety, depression, social desirability, or even IQ. Alternatively, BR conformity analysis can also be applied to between-subject measures for analyzing sample characteristics, for example.

Foundation of coping behavior rules for everyday stressful episodes

Rule-conforming behavior was studied by self-observation in natural settings using the computer-aided recording systems COMRES method described in chapter 4. The little pocket computer is started when a stressful situation - e.g. any daily hassle - occurs (event sampling). Information about the situation appraisal, coping goals and behaviors, and perceived efficiency are entered by the subject.

After self-observation the recorded episodes were first analysed on a *within-subject basis* by the *CON index* in order to establish the degree to which coping fits the rules described below. The different CON-values were also aggregated to rule-cluster measures. The CON-values were correlated *between subjects* (1) with mean rating of solving the stressful problem and of real vs. ideal coping-discrepancies also stemming from the COMRES episode recording. These indicators served as *direct* short-term indicators of efficiency. (2) They were correlated with psychological health indicators, such as depression (BDI), anxiety (STAI), psychological well-being (SDSG), positive self-concept and growth (PIL) as more *indirect* and long-term indicators. Correlations with social desirability (Crowne & Marlowe, 1960) were also tested as indicators of validity.

This initial study to establish BRs of coping focuses on a few simply structured bivariate rules of the form 'In situation X it is recommended to do Y' or 'In situation X do Y!' (Reicherts, Käslin & Perrez, 1984). The 'for' component of BR, the outcome intended by goal(s), is here conceptualized as re-equilibration of the persons' inner homeostasis, in respect to the person-environment 'transaction' (Lazarus

& Launier, 1978) - for each recorded episode by (a) reduction of the stressor, and (b) re-equilibration of emotions and/or of self-esteem.

Figure 13. Contingency patterns of coping rules A, B, E, F

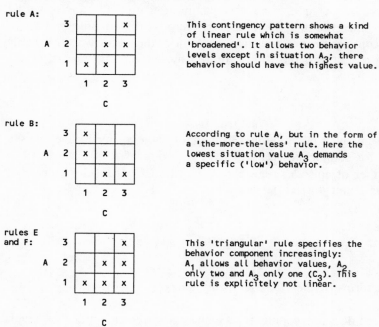

rule A:

This contingency pattern shows a kind of linear rule which is somewhat 'broadened'. It allows two behavior levels except in situation A_3; there behavior should have the highest value.

rule B:

According to rule A, but in the form of a 'the-more-the-less' rule. Here the lowest situation value A_3 demands a specific ('low') behavior.

rules E and F:

This 'triangular' rule specifies the behavior component increasingly: A_1 allows all behavior values, A_2 only two and A_3 only one (C_3). This rule is explicitly not linear.

Environment-directed coping is analysed in accordance with the following rules:

| A | The greater the controllability | --> | the more active the influence! |
| B | The greater the controllability | --> | the less evasion and avoidance! |

Self-directed coping is related to the rules:

| E | The greater the negative valence | --> | the more palliation! |
| F | The greater the probability of reoccurrence | --> | the more re-evaluation of standards! |

In completing the BR structure we should add '...if equilibration of the person's intrapsychic and social homeostasis is a goal' (Perrez, 1984). These rules were formalized by the following *contingency patterns* in figure 13.

The formalized rules are not identical with the language-based rules above. In fact it may be very complicated to find concise verbal expressions incorporating logic and the whole array of information of such rule contingency patterns. This underlines the necessity of explicitly translating a rule into the form required by the contingency pattern.

Sample

The study involved 60 students (30 men, 30 women; mean age 26; see chapter 4 for sample description) over a period of 4 to 5 weeks. The mean number of episodes registered using the COMES self-observation system was about 40 per participant.

Results

Coping in terms of the BR conformity index

Environment-directed coping rules concerning recommended behavior consequences of controllability were found to fit in about 70% of the cases. Rule A (strengthen activity!) had a mean of CON=.69 (s=.14) and rule B (diminish evasion resp. avoidance!) a mean of CON=.72 (s=.14). Self-directed coping rules reveal a lower conformity index of about 50%. Rule E (the higher valence --> the more palliative!) has a CON=.56 (s=.23) and rule F (the more probable reoccurrence --> the more re-evaluation!) a CON=.50 (s=.20).

Efficiency of rule-conforming coping behavior

The conformity indices were combined (averaged) to create an environment-directed, a self-directed and a total rule cluster score which reached a satisfactory split-half reliability level (the episodes out of the subjects' protocols, split odd-even) of r_{tt}=.78 for the environment-related cluster (A,B), r_{tt}=.84 for the self-directed cluster (E,F) and r_{tt}=.85 for the total cluster (A,B,E,F).

Coping rule clusters were then correlated with
(1) *direct coping efficiency:* a combined measure of mean level of problem solution and real-ideal coping behavior discrepancies as recorded by the subject in his COMRES stressful episodes,
(2) *psychological health:* a combined measure from the BDI, trait anxiety trait from the STAI, psychoaffective well-being (SDSG) self concept (SAF) and growth (PIL) (scales by or adapted by Becker, 1984b),
(3) *social desirability* (SD, Crowne & Marlowe, 1961) as an indicator of the validity of the rule concept and CON index.

Table 24. Conformity indices CON of different coping rules (and clusters) and their correlation with direct coping effectiveness and psychological health (N=60)

rules	A	B	E	F	A,B	E,F	A,B,E,F
CON Mean	.69	.72	.56	.50	.71	.53	.62
s	.14	.14	.23	.20	.11	.19	.11
coping efficiency	.30[c]	.32[c]	.20[a]	.38[c]	.37[c]	.33[c]	.47[d]
psychological health	.01	.13	.25[b]	.38[c]	.07	.36[c]	.34[c]

[a] $p<.10$; [b] $p<.05$; [c] $p<.01$; [d] $p<.001$; one-tailed

After obtaining the above results, all the proposed rules were related to criteria of *direct* and of *indirect or long-term* efficiency: The more the person's situation-behavior conforms to the proposed rules, the greater is the direct efficiency of coping behavior as reported in the experienced stressful episodes. Also, there are some significant correlations for combined psychological health indicators, especially for rule E and F.

The more the person's behavior conforms to the environment-directed rule cluster (A,B), the more efficient the coping ($r=.37$; $p<.01$); the psychological health indicator is not related ($r=.07$; $p>.10$).

Behavior conforming to the recommendations of the self-directed rule cluster (E,F) is positively correlated with coping efficiency ($r=.33$, $p<.01$) and the psychological health indicator ($r=.36$; $p<.01$).

By combining the mean conformity indices of the two rule clusters to a compound conformity index, the associations again become more evident: *Coping efficiency* shows a strong positive correlation with BR conformity ($r = .47$; $p < .001$), as does the psychological health indicator ($r = .34$; $p < .01$). The joint conformity index is quite independent of *social desirability* ($r = .09$).

To determine differences between *depressed* vs. non-depressed subjects we conducted extreme group comparisons between $n = 9$ persons with a score of 10 or more and $n = 11$ persons with a score of 3 or less in the BDI.

Table 25. Coping behavior rule conformity CON of depressed and non-depressed persons

| rule | conformity index CON (mean) | | | |
	depressed	non-depressed	t	p[1]
environment-directed coping:				
A	.65	.73	1.23	.12
B	.64	.77	2.10	.03[b]
C	.63	.77	2.98	.005[c]
cluster A,B,C	.64	.76	2.40	.02[b]
self-directed coping:				
D	.69	.77	1.15	.13
E	.33	.48	2.00	.03[b]
F	.45	.53	1.04	.16
cluster D,E,F	.48	.59	1.96	.04[b]
total A,B,C,D,E,F	.56	.68	3.24	.002[c]

[b] $p < .05$; [c] $p < .01$; [1] one-tailed;

The results in table 25 show the predicted differences: The level of rule conformity of the depressed persons is lower for all rules, reaching significance for some rules and for all the rule clusters. In other words, the depressed subjects 'violate' all rules to a greater or lesser extent depending on the rule than the non-depressed do.

There are other applications of the behavior rule methodology. Wiedl, Schöttner & Schöttke (1990), for example, showed that schizophrenic patients with more severe symptoms conformed less to the proposed behavior rules than patients with less severe symptoms. Schlicht, Meyer & Janssen (1990) analysed behavior rule conformity of coping with stressful situations in the context of sports psychology.

Clinical case study

Let us demonstrate the application of the BR conformity analysis within psychotherapy using the case study of a depressed young man who was in psychotherapy at the department of psychology of the University of Fribourg. At the beginning of the therapy, this patient had the typical symptoms of a reactive (neurotic) depression. His depression score (BDI=24), personality factor scores (Freiburger Persönlichkeits-Inventar FPI, scales depression and irritability increased), and other inventory data (e.g. real vs. ideal self-description, polarity profile) also clearly indicated a depression.

The analysis of his rule-oriented coping behavior towards his daily life stressors took place during the second phase of the therapy. The patient recorded 19 stressful episodes with the COMRES system (see chapter 4) using the programmed pocket computer. This period of self-observation lasted two weeks.

The patient's self-observational data were first aggregated over the stressful events he had recorded and gross means (averages) were then computed for the total of his 19 episodes; producing his global mean of controllability of the experienced situations, his global strain (negative valence), his global effort to cope with the stress by evasion/avoidance or by palliating his actual stress emotions, and so on. The following diagnostic questions were then investigated, comparing the measures of this patient with a reference group (N=60 students; as a 'norm'):

(1) Are his coping efforts globally effective? The answer is: no!

(2) Do his global coping tendencies differ from the coping tendencies of non-depressed people? For example: Does he evade/avoid stressful situations more, or does he damp down his stress emotions less than others? The answer is: no! He neither evades more than others, nor does he damp down his emotions less, overall.

(3) Does he cope with stress according to the proposed rules of adequate coping (see figure 14)? Does he behave according to the *rule B*, which recommends the degree of evasion or avoidance given the controllability of the situation? Answer: Not fully! His CON=.58 is below the reference group average (CON=.69) on the conformity index! Does his behavior conform to *rule E*? Answer: Not fully! His CON=.37 is below the mean conformity index (CON=.56) of the reference group.

A closer look at the contingency table containing the patient's stressful episodes reveals his 'violations' of the proposed coping rules (see figure 14). The shortcomings of his coping tendencies lead to the following hypothesis about the actual conditions of his ineffective coping behavior, which may relate to his depressive symptoms or to a coping style that makes him vulnerable to depression: (i) In situations of high valence, the patient does not sufficiently damp down his negative emotions. (ii) In situations of low controllability he does not try to evade/avoid stress, as rule B recommends he should. But he also attempts evasion when he perceives some controllability, instead of trying to influence the stressor.

Figure 14. Rule conformity (CON index) of coping with stress by a depressed patient

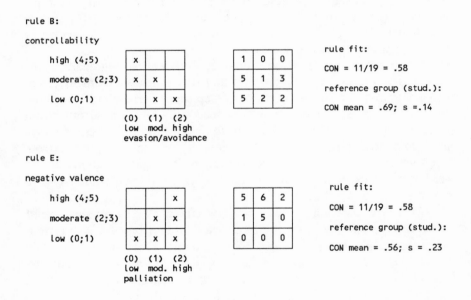

The patient does not evade/avoid excessively, but he does avoid the wrong situations! He does not generally palliate his stress emotions insufficiently - but he does it in the wrong situation! This is very important information and gives us a hint as to what the probable deficits are and where to direct our therapeutic efforts.

The way he violates the two BR's leads to the following treatment hypotheses: First we have to help this patient to realize his 'strategic errors'. For that we should use his self-observational data to analyse and illustrate his inadequate tendencies. Then we have to verify if he has the behavioral skills to evade or avoid an uncontrollable situation, and the skills to palliate his negative emotional reactions - right at the moment when they are putting him under strain and probably hindering efficient instrumental behavior. This specific intervention program was a successfully administered element of a treatment package for coping with depression.

Concluding remarks

Overall, these results seem promising. The concept of behavior rules proved useful, and the proposed methodology of BR conformity analysis was found to be viable. The conformity index obviously defines a somewhat different type of psychological variable than usual. It is a measure condensing several within-subject observations on at least two dimensions (situation antecedent; behavioral consequent) relative to an explicit structure. It may correspond to either rational or intersubjectively founded 'nomopragmatic' knowledge.

This approach should provide the possibility of transforming empirical evidence from studies of daily life behavior into rules stated in the form of nomopragmatic propositions containing situation antecedents (A), characteristics of the chosen behaviors (C) and the quality of outcome in relation to the goals (O) (For epistemological problems of the empirical foundation of rules see Bunge, 1967; or Perrez & Patry, 1982). It will be interesting to follow this path and to translate other of the more striking 'rules of thumb' and heuristics of everyday life into behavior rules or 'technological rules' in Bunge's terms.

Case studies V:
Behavior rules analysis and some final reflections

Behavior rule analysis of Evelyn and Harry's coping behavior

It is interesting to analyse the episodes of Harry and Evelyn with regard to their conformity to behavior rules of coping. The lost young man rated his getting lost by the following characteristics (see also table 11; situational antecedents a; behavioral consequents c):

Controllability rather high (a=4), changeability low (=1), negative valence high (=4), and probability of reoccurrence low (=1). He describes a high instrumental activity (=2) and search for support (=2); asking for information, trying to get a taxi, finally asking the car driver for help. And he indicates low passivity (=0), although for some moments he didn't know what to do and therefore waited and hesitated. So he is correct in rating activity more highly than passivity.

In the contingency table for rule A, Harry's episode is assigned to the top right cell, which conforms to the rule: his coping behavior concerning instrumental activity was therefore consistent with the proposed rule. He also reported high valence for the episode, which should be responded to with some intensive palliative action, calming self-instructions, breathing control or attempts at relaxation. These are preconditions for good mental problem solving and for seizing the opportunity (as Harry did) of perceiving the car driver and asking him at just the right moment, and in the right way. For rule E his ratings belong to the top middle cell, which doesn't conform to the rule. Apparently his moderate palliative action this time was enough to allow him to act; he successfully coped with the situation, without conforming to all the rules.

Concerning rule F (reoccurrence --> re-evaluation) his episode is situated in the bottom centre cell on the contingency table. When probability of reoccurrence is low, the rule is not specific; he can make strong or weak efforts of re-evaluation, positive thinking or philosophical acceptance. The rule recommends the re-evaluation of the situation only if their reoccurrence is expected. Therefore his coping behavior also conforms to rule F.

Because he wanted to cope with the situation and reduce stress, all the rules applied to his episode and therefore their recommendations were relevant to him. This episode demonstrates that total rule conformity is not a sufficient and necessary condition for successful coping in every single case. Instead, it gives an adequate and reasonable recommendation for behavior, which in general is efficient. This aspect of the valence-palliation rule also illustrates, why rule conformity is rarely perfect (100%).

Figure 14: Rule conformity analysis of Harry's stressful episodes

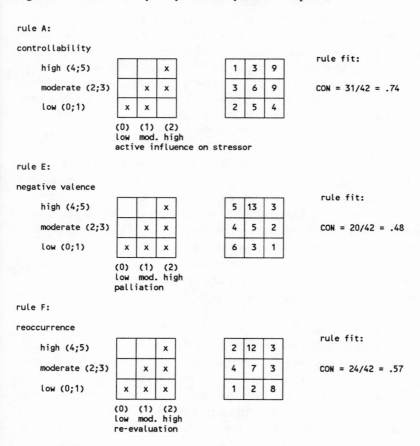

The proposed behavior rules reflect more heuristic strategies, like the cook's recipe which doesn't guarantee a fantastic meal. But meals can still be fantastic even if you don't do exactly what is recommended in the recipe.

His total rule-conformity index refers to the whole sample of situations he reported by means of the COMRES system (including the episode just analysed). His rule-conformity index for rule A is about 74%, for rule E 48%, and rule F 57%. Compared with the sample of N=60 students, all his rule conformity indices are average. The example shows that the coping behavior of one episode which does not conform to a rule doesn't have to produce conspicuous rule-violation effects.

All in all, the young man's coping-behavior rule conformity is an important factor promoting his *coping success* (high problem solving tendency and low behavior discrepancies), which he reports in his COMRES self-assessment. In the long run he will probably profit from this, having fewer psychological and psychosomatic symptoms, and being more content with his life.

Evelyn's coping with the earring episode also conformed to the rules. Controllability of the final situations was very low, and therefore reducing activity and instrumentally giving up conformed to rule A. She perceived the situation as very stressful, and she actively tried to calm herself and to comfort herself (intensive palliation; corresponding to rule E) and to re-evaluate and actively re-orientate herself concerning the important lost object. Despite the low probability of its reoccurrence, her coping conformed to rule F.

Some final reflections

On finishing our sketch about the application of theoretical ideas, diagnostic instruments and empirical results to the two individuals, we wish to make it plain that it was the purpose of the case studies to show how a theoretical framework can help to interpret *the person's real life experiences* and can reduce an event to theoretically relevant terms. This reconstruction becomes a more precise facet, when the concepts and variables of the theory are operationalized by measurement procedures and/or diagnostic instruments. This procedure makes new information available about the person, if the individual's value can be related to the distribution of the values of his reference group or can be compared with 'ideal' values, however they may be founded.

Furthermore, we wanted to illustrate the kinds of information which can be gained from empirical group studies in order to achieve a deeper understanding of individuals. This understanding is based on evidence which is far from conclusive. A scientific view of the individual implies the selection of some aspects of reality, the putting up with uncertainty, and the ascription of properties in terms of probabilities. As the claim to describe individuality in its totality is rather a goal of certain novelists, certainty on the other hand is a characteristic of everyday psychology. Scientific understanding of human behavior is achieved by reducing the complexity of the behavior stream and by trying to estimate the probabilities of error in making diagnostic and therapeutic conclusions concerning the individual.

12. Conclusion

In the previous chapters we have attempted to conceptualize some psychological aspects of stress and coping within the framework of a situation-behavior theory. We have described two new assessment instruments and the empirical results obtained in line with the theoretical assumptions. An initial issue concerned the postulate that adaptation processes can be analysed advantageously if stress *episodes* are chosen as units for analysis. This may be true also for macro-events such as critical life events which can be interpreted as a sequence of micro-events, i.e. episodes. Episodes have a structure.

Situational features play a particular role if this structure is to be modelled. The dynamic of the episode, i.e. its process, is - within limits - predictable by specific parameters. Furthermore, we postulated that it is, in principle, possible to validate propositions on *appropriate coping behavior* taking into consideration situational features which define the coping task. We described two new *assessment methods*. Both have been developed to assess stress and coping behavior within the sketched theoretical framework.

Episodes as units of analysis

Unlike the critical life event research and some other research approaches to coping with stress, we have chosen the *stressful episode* as our research unit. We consider critical life events as a sequence of stress episodes which represent quite heterogenous coping-tasks, depending on situational features. The macro-event generates a series of heterogenous micro-events. Such stressful episodes constitute a level of conceptualization which is more 'molecular' than critical life events, but less molecular than, for example, approaches dealing with information-processing or with the role of cognitive processes for micro-regulation of emotions.

Theoretical assumptions concerning the coping process

The psychological description of coping episodes presupposes theoretical assumptions about the conditions influencing the process. The predictions relate specific features of the situations and their appraisal with emotional and coping behavior. Objective controllability, changeability and other factors and their subjective appraisal have been considered as important for the prediction of emotional and coping responses.

Assessment of coping within the episode-approach

The episode-approach needs new assessment methods to observe coping behavior. Two instruments have been described in the previous chapters, one working with hypothetical situations which simulate processes of stress encounters; the other focuses on self-observation in the natural setting. Both allow the collection of coping- and adaptation-relevant psychological data.

What does 'adaptation-relevant' or 'appropriate' coping mean?

We would suggest that within a single coping episode a coping response is appropriate if the response takes into account the demands of the concrete situation. Judgements about the functional relevance of coping responses presupposes knowledge of coping-relevant objective features of the stressor or the situation. This knowledge enables us to evaluate to what extent a response meets the demands of the situation. We assume that appropriate coping can be characterized firstly by a correspondence between objective features of the situation and their cognitive representation by the subject and second by a correspondence between cognitive representation/appraisal and the coping response.

A coping task can be divided into two subtasks: the first consists of an accurate perception (within certain limits) of characteristics of a stressor relevant to coping (controllability etc.), and the second of the availability of an appropriate response as a function of perception (e.g. controllable stressor --> active influence; uncontrollable stressor --> attitude and/or goal change). Dysfunctional coping can be caused by perceptional deficits and/or by the non-availability of coping competencies in spite of a correct perception.

We proposed examples of behavioral rules which recommend to the actor specific response types depending on situational features and we described a rationale for the empirical foundation of such rules. We also proposed a methodology to measure the relative conformity of the coping behavior of a person in terms of the behavioral rules.

We see this approach as having major implications for *health promotion*. This is because new health interventions can be planned according to our increasing knowledge about what will constitute an adaptation response to real life stressors. It seems to us that adaptive responding to real life stressors will have a significant influence on health.

Empirical evidence

Most of the empirical findings are in line with our theoretical assumptions. Even if not all hypotheses are confirmed, only a few results contradict the assumptions. As expected objectively more controllable situations are perceived as more controllable and are followed with a higher probability of active instrumental behavior and less evasive or passive tendencies. Depressed people differ from non-depressed in underestimating controllability and in preferring less instrumental activity. Also patterns of emotions are connected with objective and/or subjectively perceived situational features. Assumptions of the situation-behavior approach improve the predictability of stress and coping behavior in natural settings, using self-observation data.

Other results show that stress and coping tendencies assessed in everyday episodes are also related to indicators of mental health. This is also true for coping tendencies which take into account adaptation-relevant (subjective perceptions of) features of the situations - as conceptualized by the behavioral rules.

Although the previous chapters have not always spelt out precisely the implication for health psychology, nevertheless the implications are clear and unambiguous. There is now clear evidence that environmental stressors and coping behaviors have a major impact on physiological functioning especially that which mediates various diseases, e.g. via hormone and immune feedback systems (e.g. Gilbert, 1989; Henry & Stephans, 1977).

Some problems

With regard to the *situation*, the features we proposed - controllability, changeability, valence and reoccurrence - seem to reflect essential aspects of the complex antecedent constellation called a 'stressful situation'. But other features may also be of interest, e.g. the conditions which have caused the stressful situation. Another issue, not yet fully resolved, concerns the *configurations* of situational features relevant to stress and coping behavior. First empirical results, e.g. some cluster analyses bode well for a further theoretical elaboration of such configurations of situational characteristics. This issue also concerns the behavior rule approach.

The proposed taxonomy of *coping behavior* is basic and economic. But it is also global. The proposed functional classes of situation-oriented (internal and/or external), representation-oriented and evaluation/volition-oriented coping behavior allow one to describe important coping variants. However, for certain issues it may be necessary to differentiate the *coping repertoires* of the three classes.

In several studies we used *health* as a criterion for adaptation. We referred to this meta-construct only in some aspects. The empirical studies reported here consider mental health only and they focus (with some exceptions) on certain indicators such as psychological well-being, anxiety, depression, positive purpose in life and self-acceptance. It is desirable to know more about other aspects of mental health like 'hardiness', or 'anger-in', 'anger-out' or 'anger-control' and also about the relationship between mental health and somatic health parameters. These areas are currently being studied.

Methodologically, there is a lack of experimental evidence about the theoretical assumptions of the situation-behavior model, with the exception of the 'quasi-experimental' analysis of the impact of situation and process factors on stress and coping responses (chapter 3). There is a need for sophisticated designs to realize different situational characteristics within the laboratory setting which allow their influence on perception, stress and coping behavior to be tested (Does intransparency lead to more search for information? Under what circumstances?). In the same way, the - immediate - effects of coping responses on the outcome of an episode (problem solving and emotional regulation) need to be tested. A first experimental study has just been completed applying the above theoretical principles for studying coping behavior in dyadic interaction (Bodenmann & Perrez, 1991).

There is another methodological approach which is, so far, only in its beginning, which involves improving certain tendencies of stress and coping behavior by specific intervention strategies into better tendencies (or competencies). Such treatments still require elaboration and evaluation concerning their short-term effects in single episodes, and their long-term influences on health (by follow-up studies). Whereas experimental studies improve the evidence concerning the *lawfulness of theoretical assumptions*, the treatment evaluation studies help to improve the *practical usefulness* of the situation-behavior model, as illustrated in the HIV treatment study in chapter 8.

A conceptual characteristic of the approach is the decomposition of macro-episodes - as critical life events or chronic stressors - into microepisodes, with real life situations and circumscribed behaviors. This is a *analytic* strategy, which as the results show, is fruitful and allows an *integration*: to relate different aspects of situations, appraisals, emotions, and behaviors with each other and to analyse them in a more comprehensive way.

References

Abramson, L.Y, Seligman, M.E.P., & Teasdale, J. (1978). Learned helplessness in humans: Critique and reformulation. *Journal of Abnormal Psychology, 87,* 49-74.

Alloy, L.B., & Abramson, L.Y. (1979). Judgement of contingency in depressed or non-depressed students: Sadder but wiser? *Journal of Experimental Psychology (General), 108,* 441-485.

Alloy, L.B., & Abramson, L.Y. (1982). Learned helplessness, depression, and the illusion of control. *Journal of Personality and Social Psychology, 42,* 1114-1126.

Andrews, G., Tennant, C., Hewson, D., & Schonell, M. (1978). The relation of social factors to physical and psychiatric illness. *American Journal of Epidemiology, 108,* 27-35.

Antonovsky, A. (1979). *Health, Stress, and Coping.* San Francisco: Jossey-Bass.

Arnold, M.B. (1960). *Emotion and personality* (Vol. 1 & 2). New York: Columbia University Press.

Bandura, A. (1977). Self-efficacy: Toward an unifying theory of behavioral change. *Psychological Review, 84,* 191-215.

Baron, R.M., & Kenny, D.A. (1986). The moderator-mediator variable distinction in social psychological research: Conceptual, strategic, and statistical considerations. *Journal of Personality and Social Psychology, 51,* 1173-1182.

Beck, A.T. (1972). *Depression.* Philadelphia: University of Pennsylvania Press.

Beck, A.T. (1976). *Cognitive therapy and the emotional disorders.* New York: International Universities Press.

Beck, A.T. (1991). Cognitive therapy - a 30-year retrospective. *American Psychologist, 46,* 368-375.

Beck, A.T., Ward, C.H., Mendelson, M., Mock, J., & Erbaugh, J. (1961). An inventory for measuring depression. *Archives of General Psychiatry, 4,* 53-63.

Becker, P. (1981). Neuere psychologische Ätiologietheorien der Depression und Angst. In W.R. Minsel & R. Scheller (Hrsg.), *Brennpunkte der Klinischen Psychologie, Prävention* (S.25-62). München: Kösel.

Becker, P. (1984a). *Bewältigungsverhalten und Psychische Gesundheit* (Trierer Psychologische Berichte 11, 5). Trier: Universität, Psychologisches Institut.

Becker, P. (1984b). *Fragebögen zur Selbstaktualisierung (SAF) und zur seelischen Gesundheit (SG).* Unveröff. Manuskript, Universität Trier, Psychologisches Institut.

Becker, P. (1986). Theoretischer Rahmen. In P. Becker & B. Minsel (Hrsg.), *Psychologie der seelischen Gesundheit* (Bd. 2) (S. 1-90). Göttingen: Hogrefe.

Becker, P. (1991). Theoretische Grundlagen. In A. Abele & P. Becker (Hrsg.), *Wohlbefinden. Theorie-Empirie-Diagnostik* (S. 13-49). München: Juventa.

Billings, A.G., & Moos, R.H. (1981). The role of coping responses and social resources in attenuating the impact of stressful life events. *Journal of Behavioral Medicine, 4,* 139-157.

Billings, A.G., & Moos, R.H. (1982). Stressful life events and symptoms: A longitudinal model. *Health Psychology, 1,* 99-117.

Blöschl, L. (1982). Stress and stress-reducing factors in depression: A reinforcement-oriented analysis. In J. Boulougouris (ed.), *Learning theory approaches to psychiatry* (p. 231-236). New York: Wiley.

Bodenmann, G., & Perrez, M. (1991). *Experimentell induzierter Stress in dyadischen Interaktionen (Darstellung des EISI-Experiments)* (Forschungsbericht Nr. 82). Freiburg/Schweiz: Universität, Psychologisches Institut.

Boss, P.G., McCubbin, H.I., & Lester, G. (1979). The corporate executive wife's coping patterns in response to routine husband-father absence. *Family Process, 18,* 70-86.

Braukmann, W., & Filipp, S.-H. (1983). *Die "Skala zur Erfassung des Bewältigungsverhaltens" (SEBV): Bericht über Aufbau, Gütekennzeichen und differentielle Zusammenhänge mit Merkmalen bedeutsamer Lebensereignisse* (Forschungsbericht Nr. 27 aus dem Projekt Entwicklungspsychologie des Erwachsenenalters). Trier: Universität.

Brewin, C.R., & Furnham, A. (1986). Attributional versus preattributional variables in self-esteem and depression: A comparison and test of learned helplessness theory. *Journal of Personality and Social Psychology, 50,* 1013-1020.

Brown, G.W., Bifulco, A., & Harris, T.O. (1987). Life events, vulnerability and onset of depression: Some refinements. *British Journal of Psychiatry, 150,* 30-42.

Bühler, K. (1927). *Die Krise der Psychologie.* Jena: Gustav Fischer.

Bunge, M. (1967). *Scientific research. The search for truth* (Vol. II). Berlin: Springer.

Cantor, N., Mischel, W., & Schwartz, J.C. (1982). A prototype analysis of psychological situations. *Cognitive Psychology, 14,* 45-77.

Casadontes, P.P., Des Jarlais, D., Smith, T., Novatt, A., & Hemdahl, P. (1986). Psychological and behavioral impact of learning HTLV-III/LAV antibody test results (Poster 444). *Proceedings of the II International Conference in Acquired Immunodeficiency Syndrome (AIDS)* (p. 163). Paris, France: Voyage Conseil.

Chevrier, E. (1987). *Coping et adaptation de personnes atteintes du virus du SIDA issues du groupe a risques des toxicomanes.* Mémoire de licence (non publié). Fribourg/Suisse, Université.

Chuang, H.T., Devins, G.M., Hunsley, J., & Gill, M.J. (1989). Psychological distress and well-being among gay and bisexual men with human immunodeficiency virus infection. *The American Journal of Psychiatry, 146,* 876-880.

Coates, T.J., Stall, R., Mandel, J.S., Boccellari, A., Sorensen, J.L., Morales, E.F., Morin, S.F., Wiley, J.A., & McKusick, L. (1987). AIDS: A psychosocial research agenda. *Annals of Behavioral Medicine, 9,* 21-28.

Cohen, M.A., & Weisman, H.W. (1986). A biopsychological approach to AIDS. *Psychosomatics, 27,* 245-249.

Coombs, R.H., & Goldman, L.J. (1973). Maintenance and discontinuity of coping mechanisms in an intensive care unit. *Social Problems, 20,* 342-355.

Coyne, J.C., & Gotlib, I.H. (1983). The role of cognition in depression: A critical appraisal. *Psychological Bulletin, 94,* 472-505.

Crowne, D.P., & Marlowe, D. (1960). A new scale of social desirability independent of psychopathology. *Journal of Consulting Psychology, 24,* 349-354.

Crumbaugh, J.C., & Maholick, L.T. (1972). Eine experimentelle Untersuchung im Bereich der Existenzanalyse: Ein psychometrischer Ansatz zu Viktor Frankls Konzept der neogenen Neurose. In N. Petrilowitsch (Hrsg.), *Die Sinnfrage in der Psychotherapie* (S. 467-482). Darmstadt: Wissenschaftliche Buchgesellschaft.

Crumbaugh, J.C., & Maholick, L.T. (1981). *Manual for the Purpose in Life Test.* Indiana: Psychometric Affiliates.

DeLongis, A., Lazarus, R.S., & Folkman, S. (1988). The impact of daily stress on health and mood: Psychological and social resources as mediators. *Journal of Personality and Social Psychology, 54,* 486-495.

Ebel, R.L. (1962). Content standard test scores. *Educational and Psychological Measurement, 22,* 15-25.

Ehlers, A., Margraf, J., & Roth, W.T. (1988). Selective information processing, interoception, and panic attacks. In I. Hand & H.U. Wittchen (eds.), *Panic and phobias 2* (pp.129-148). Berlin: Springer.

Ekehammar, B. (1974). Interactionism in psychology from a historical perspective. *Psychological Bulletin, 81,* 765-784.

Ellis, A. (1979). The theory of rational-emotive therapy. In A. Ellis & J.M. Whiteley (Eds.), Theoretical and empirical foundations of rational-emotive therapy (p. 33-60). Monterey: Brooks/Cole.

Endler, N.S., & Magnusson, D. (eds.) (1976). *Interactional psychology and personality.* Washington, D.C.: Hemisphere.

Endler, N.S., & Okada, M. (1975). A multidimensional measure of trait anxiety: The S-R inventory of trait anxiousness. *Journal of Consulting and Clinical Psychology, 43,* 319-329.

Endler, N., Hunt, J. McV., & Rosenstein, A.J. (1962). An S-R inventory of anxiousness. *Psychological Monographs, 76, No. 17.*

Ericson, K.A., & Simon, H.A. (1980). Verbal reports as data. *Psychological Review, 87,* 215-251.

Fenz, W.D., & Epstein, S. (1962). Measurement of approach-avoidance conflict along a stimulus dimension by a thematic apperception test. *Journal of Personality, 30,* 613-632.

Firth, J., & Brewin, C. (1982). Attributions and recovery from depression: A preliminary study using cross-lagged correlation analysis. *British Journal of Clinical Psychology, 21,* 219-230.

Fisher, S. (1984). *Stress and the perception of control.* London: Erlbaum.

Fisher, S. (1986). *Stress and strategy.* London: Erlbaum.

Fisher, S., & Elder, L. (1990). Epidemiological problem analysis: A new approach to the measurement of stress. *Stress Medicine,6,*189-200.

Folkman, S. (1982). An approach to the measurement of coping. In Journal of Occupational Behavior, 3, 95-107.

Folkman, S. (1984). Personal control and stress and coping processes: A theoretical analysis. *Journal of Personality and Social Psychology, 46,* 839-852.

Folkman, S., & Lazarus, R.S. (1980). An analysis of coping in a middle-aged-community sample. *Journal of Health and Social Behavior, 21,* 219-239.

Folkman, S., & Lazarus, R.S. (1986). Stress processes and depressive symptomatology. *Journal of Abnormal Psychology, 95,* 107-113.

Folkman, S., & Lazarus, R.S. (1988). Coping as a mediator of emotion. *Journal of Personality and Social Psychology, 54,* 466-475.

Folkman, S., & Lazarus, R.S. (1988). *Manual for the Ways of Coping Questionnaire.* Palo Alto, CA: Consulting Psychologists Press.

Folkman, S., Lazarus, R.S., Gruen, R.J., & DeLongis, A. (1986). Appraisal, coping, health status, and psychological symptoms. *Journal of Personality and Social Psychology, 50,* 571-579.

Folkman, S., Lazarus, R.S., Dunkel-Schetter, Ch., DeLongis, A., & Gruen, R.J. (1986). Dynamics of a stressful encounter: Cognitive appraisal, coping, and encounter outcomes. *Journal of Personality and Social Psychology, 50,* 992-1003.

Fricke, R. (1974). *Kriteriumsorientierte Leistungsmessung.* Stuttgart: Kohlhammer.

Frigo, M.A., Zones, J.S., Besson, D.R., Rutherford, G.W. Echenberg, D.F., & O'Malley, O.M. (1986). The impact of structured counseling in acute adverse psychiatric reactions associated with LAV/HTLV-III antibody testing (Abstract 284). *Proceedings of the 114th Annual Meeting of American Public Health Association.* Las Vegas, Nevada.

Frijda, N (1986). *The emotions.* Cambridge and New York: Cambridge University Press.

Garber, J., Miller, S.M., & Ambramson, L.Y. (1980). On the distinction between anxiety and depression: Perceived control, certainty, and probability of goal attainment. In J. Garber & M.E.P. Seligman (eds.), *Human helplessness* (pp. 131-172). New York: Academic Press.

Glaser, R. (1963). Instructional technology and the measurement of learning outcomes: Some questions. *American Psychologist, 18,* 519-521.

Gilbert, Paul (1989). *Human nature and suffering.* London and Hillsdale: Erlbaum.

Gilbert, Paul (1992). *Depression: Types, concepts, and theories. An evolutionary synthesis on the themes of power and belonging.* London: Erlbaum.

Golin, S., Sweeney, P.D., & Schaeffer, D.E. (1981). The causality of causal attribution in depression: A cross-lagged panel correlation analysis. *Journal of Abnormal Psychology, 90,* 14-22.

Grant, I., Sweetwood, H.L., Yager, J., & Gerst, M. (1981). Quality of life events in relation to psychiatric symptoms. *Archives of General Psychiatry, 38,* 335-339.

Gray-Toft, P., & Anderson, J.G. (1981). The Nursing Stress Scale: Development of an instrument. *Journal of Behavioral Assessment, 3,* 11-23.

Gruen, R.J., Folkman, S., & Lazarus, R.S. (1988). Centrality and individual differences in the meaning of daily hassles. *Journal of Personality, 56,* 743-762.

Hammen, C.L., & Cochran, S.D. (1981). Cognitive correlates of life stress and depression in college students. *Journal of Abnormal Psychology, 90,* 23-27.

Hänggi, D., & Schedle, A. (1987). *Induzierte Imagination als methodisches Paradigma zur Erfassung von Stresserleben und Stressbewältigung* (Forschungsbericht Nr. 63). Freiburg/ Schweiz: Universität, Psychologisches Institut.

Harlow, H.F. (1953). Mice, monkeys, men and motives. *Psychological Review, 60,* 23-32.

Harris, R.D., Bond, M.J., & Turnbull, R. (1990). Nursing stress and stress reduction in palliative care. *Palliative Medicine, 4,* 191-196.

Hautzinger, M. (1980). Antidepressive Bewältigungsmechanismen. In R. de Jong, N. Hoffmann & M. Linden (Eds.), *Verhaltensmodifikation bei Depressionen* (S. 72-81). München: Urban & Schwarzenberg.

Heider, F. (1958). *The psychology of interpersonal relations.* New York: Wiley.

Hempel, C.G. (1965). *Aspects of scientific explanation and other essays in the philosophy of science.* New York: The Free Press.

Henry, J.P., & Stephens, P.M. (1977). *Stress, health, and the social environment.* New York:Springer.

Hildebrand, D.K., Laing, J.D., & Rosenthal, H. (1977). *Prediction analysis of cross classifications.* New York: Wiley.

Holland, J.G., & Skinner, B.F. (1961). *The analysis of behavior.* New York: McGraw Hill.

Holmes, T.H., & Rahe, R.H. (1967). The social readjustment rating scale. *Journal of Psychosomatic Research, 11,* 213-218.

Horowitz, M.J., & Becker, S.S. (1971). The impulsion to repeat trauma: Experimental study of intrusive thinking after stress. *Journal of Nervous and Mental Disease, 152,* 32-40.

Horowitz, M.J., & Wilner, N. (1976). Stress films, emotion, and cognitive response. *Archives of General Psychiatry, 33,* 1339-1344.

Houston, B.K. (1982). Trait anxiety and cognitive coping behavior. In H.W. Krohne & L. Laux (Hrsg.), *Achievement, stress, and anxiety* (pp. 195-206). Washington: Hemisphere.

Ilfeld, F.W. (1980). Coping styles of Chicago adults: Effectiveness. *Archives of General Psychiatry, 37,* 1239-1243.

Jacobson, S.F. (1983). Stresses and coping strategies of neonatal intensive care unit nurses. *Research in Nursing and Health, 6,* 33-40.

Jäger, H. (1988). Die psychosoziale Betreuung von AIDS- und AIDS-Vorfeldpatienten. *Internist, 29,* 97-102.

Janis, I.L. (1958). *Psychological stress.* New York: McGraw-Hill.

Joseph, J.G., Emmons, C.A., Kessler, R.C., Ostrow, D.G., & Phair, J. (1985). Changes in sexual behavior of gay men: Relationships to perceived stress and psychological symptomatology. In *Proceedings of the First International Conference on the Acquired Immune Deficiency Syndrome (AIDS)* (p. 160). Atlanta, GA.

Kanfer, F., & Hagerman, S.M. (1984). Behavior therapy and the information processing paradigm. In S. Reiss & R.R. Hobtzin (Eds.), *Theoretical issues in behavior therapy.* New York: Academic Press 1984.

Keane, A., Ducette, J,, & Adler, D.C. (1985). Stress in ICU and non-ICU nurses. *Nursing Research, 34,* 231-236.

Kelley, H.H. (1972). *Causal schemata and the attribution process.* New York: General Learning Press.

Kelly, G.A. (1955). *The psychology of personal constructs.* New York: Norton.

Klauer, K.-J. (1984). Kontentvalidität. *Diagnostica, 30,* 1-23.

Klauer, K.-J. (1987). *Kriteriumsorientierte Tests.* Göttingen: Hogrefe.

Klauer, T., & Filipp, S.-H. (1987). *Der 'Fragebogen zur Erfassung von Formen der Krankheitsbewältigung' (FEKB): Kurzbeschreibung der Verfahrens* (Forschungsbericht aus dem Projekt 'Psychologie der Krankheitsbewältigung' Nr. 13). Trier: Universität.

Klauer, T., Ferring, D., & Filipp, S.-H. (1989). Zur Spezifität der Bewältigung schwerer körperlicher Erkrankungen: Eine vergleichende Analyse dreier diagnostischer Gruppen. *Zeitschrift für Klinische Psychologie, 18,* 144-158.

Krantz, S., & Hammen, C.L. (1979). Assessment of cognitive bias in depression. *Journal of Abnormal Psychology, 88,* 611-619.

Krohne, H.W. (1986). Coping with stress. Dispositions, strategies, and the problem of measurement. In M.H. Appley & R. Trumbull (eds.), *Dynamics of stress* (pp. 209-234). New York: Plenum Press.

Krohne, H.W. (1990). Personality as a mediator between objective events and their subjective representation. *Psychological Inquiry, 1,* 26- 29.

Krohne, H.W., Rösch, W., & Kürsten, F. (1989). Die Erfassung von Angstbewältigung in physisch bedrohlichen Situationen. *Zeitschrift für Klinische Psychologie, 18,* 230-242.

Landeweerd, J.A., & Boumans, N.P. (1988). Work satisfaction, health, and stress: A study of Dutch nurses. *Work and Stress, 2,* 17-26.

Lang, P.J., Levin, D.N., Miller, G.A., & Kozak, M.J. (1983). Fear behavior, fear imagery, and the psychophysiology of emotion: The problem of affective response integration. *Journal of Abnormal Psychology, 92,* 276-306.

Laux, L., & Vossel, G. (1982). Paradigms in stress research: Laboratory versus field and trait versus process. In L. Goldberg & S. Breznitz (eds.), *Handbook of stress. Theoretical and clinical aspects* (pp. 203-211). New York/London: The Free Press.

Laux, L., & Weber, H. (1987). Person-centered coping research. *European Journal of Personality, 1,* 193-214.

Laux, L., & Weber, H. (1990). Bewältigung von Emotionen. In K.R. Scherer (Hrsg.), *Psychologie der Emotion* (S. 560-629). Göttingen: Hogrefe.

Laux, L., & Weber, H. (1991). Presentation of self in coping with anger and anxiety: An intentional approach. *Anxiety research, 3,* 233-255.

Laux, L., Glanzmann, P., Schaffner, P., & Spielberger, C.D. (1981). *Das State-Trait-Angstinventar. Theoretische Grundlagen und Handanweisung.* Weinheim: Beltz.

Lazarus, R.S. (1966). *Psychological stress and the coping process.* New York: McGraw-Hill.

Lazarus, R.S. (1982). Thoughts on the relation between emotion and cognition. *American Psychologist, 37,* 1019-1024.

Lazarus, R.S. (1983). The costs and benefits of denial. In S. Breznitz (ed.), *The denial of stress* (pp.1-30). New York: International Universities Press.

Lazarus, R.S. (1984). On the primacy of cognition. *American Psychologist, 39,* 124-129.

Lazarus, R.S. (1990). Author's response. *Psychological Inquiry, 1,* 41-51.

Lazarus, R.S. (1991). Cognition and motivation in emotion. *American Psychologist, 46,* 352-367.

Lazarus, R.S., & Folkman, S. (1984). *Stress, appraisal, and coping.* New York: Springer.

Lazarus, R.S., & Folkman, S. (1987). Transactional theory and research on emotions and coping. In L. Laux & G. Vossel (eds.), Personality in biographical stress and coping research. *European Journal of Personality, 1,* 141-169.

Lazarus, R.S., & Launier, R. (1978). Stress-related transactions between person and environment. In L.A. Pervin & M. Lewis (eds.), *Perspectives in interactional psychology* (pp. 287-327). New York: Plenum Press.

Lazarus, R.S., & Smith, C.A. (1988). Knowledge and appraisal in the cognition-emotion relationship. *Cognition and Emotion, 2,* 281-300.

Lazarus, R.S., Kanner, A.D., & Folkman, S. (1980). Emotions: A cognitive-phenomenological analysis. In R. Plutchik & H. Kellermann (eds.), *Emotions. Theory, research, and experience* (Vol. 1): Theories of emotion (pp. 189-217). New York: Academic Press.

Lazarus, R.S., DeLongis, A., Folkman, S., & Gruen, R. (1985). Stress and adaptational outcomes. The problem of confounded measures. *American Psychologist, 40,* 770-779.

Lazarus, R.S., Speisman, J.C., Mordkoff, A.M., & Davison, L.A. (1962). A laboratory study of psychological stress produced by a motion picture film (Whole No. 553). *Psychological Monographs: General and Applied, 76.*

Lazarus, R.S., Speisman, J.C., & Mordkoff, A.M. (1963). The relationship between autonomic indicators of psychological stress: Heart rate and skin conductance. *Psychosomatic Medicine, 25,* 19-30.

Lebart, L.; Morineau, A., & Lambert, Th. (1987). *SPAD.N: Statistical package for the analysis of data.* Sèvres: Cisia.

Lefebvre, M.F. (1981). Cognitive distortion and cognitive errors in depressed psychiatric and low back pain patients. *Journal of Consulting and Clinical Psychology, 49,* 517-525.

Leventhal, H., & Scherer, K.R. (1987). The relationship of emotion to cognition: A functional approach to a semantic controversy. *Cognition and Emotion, 1,* 3-28.

Lewin, K.A. (1935). *A dynamic theory of personality* (Trans., K.E. Zener & D.K. Adams). New York: McGraw-Hill.

Lewinsohn, P.M.; Antonuccio, D.O.; Steinmetz, J.L., & Teri, L. (1984). *The coping with depression course.* Eugene: Castalia.

Lienert, G.A. (1978). *Verteilungsfreie Methoden der Biostatistik* (Bd. 2). Meisenheim/Glan: Anton Hain.

Lord, F.M., & Novick, M.R. (Eds). (1968). *Statistical theories of mental test scores.* Reading, Mass.: Addison-Wesley.

Lück, H.E., & Timaeus, E. (1969). Skalen zur Messung manifester Angst (MAS) und sozialer Wünschbarkeit (SDS-E). *Diagnostica, 15,* 134-141.

Magnusson, D. (1980). Personality in an interactional paradigm of research. *Zeitschrift für Differentielle und Diagnostische Psychologie, 1,* 17-34.

Magnusson, D., & Endler, N.S. (1977). *Personality at the crossroads: Current issues in interactional psychology.* Hillsdale, N.J.: Erlbaum.

Magnusson, D., & Stattin, H. (1982). Methods for studying stressful situations. In H.W. Krohne & L. Laux (eds.), *Achievement, stress, and anxiety* (pp. 317-331). Washington: Hemisphere.

McClelland, D.C. (1951). *Personality.* New York: Sloane.

McCrae, R.R. (1989). Situational determinants of coping. In B.N. Carpenter (Ed.), *Personal coping: Theory, research, and application.* New York: Praeger.

McFarlane, A., Norman, G., Streiner, D., Roy, R., & Scott, D. (1980). A longitudinal study of the influence of the psychosocial environment on health status: A preliminary report. *Journal of Health and Social Behavior, 21,* 124-133.

McGrath, J.E. (1976). Stress and behavior in organizations. In M.D. Dunette (ed.), *Handbook of industrial and organizational psychology* (pp. 1351-1394). Chicago: Rand McNally.

McGrath, J.E. (1982). Methodological problems in research on stress. In H.W. Krohne & L. Laux (eds.), *Achievement, stress, and anxiety* (pp. 19-48). Washington: Hemisphere.

Mechanic, D. (1962). *Students under stress.* New York: Free Press.

Menaghan, E.G. (1982). Measuring coping effectiveness: A panel analysis of marital problems and coping effects. *Journal of Health and Social Behavior, 23,* 220-234.

Michael, W.B. (1966). An interpretation of the coefficients of predictive validity and of determination in terms of the proportions of correct inclusions or exclusions in cells of a fourfold table. *Educational and Psychological Measurement, 26,* 419-426.

Miller, G., Galanter, E., & Pribram, K. (1960). *Plans and the structure of behavior.* New York: Holt, Rinehart & Winston.

Miller, S.M. (1979). Coping with impending stress: Psychophysiological and cognitive correlates of choice. *Psychophysiology, 16,* 572-581.

Mischel, W. (1968). *Personality and assessment.* New York: Wiley.

Mischel, W. (1973). Toward a cognitive social learning theory of personality. *Psychological Review, 80,* 252-283.

Monat, A., Averill, J.R., & Lazarus, R.S. (1972). Anticipatory stress and coping reactions under various conditions of uncertainty. *Journal of Personality and Social Psychology, 24,* 237-253.

Morin, S.F., & Batchelor, W.F. (1984). Responding to the psychological crisis of AIDS. *Public Health Reports, 99,* 4-9.

Murphy, G. (1947). *Personality: A biosocial approach to origins and structure.* New York-London.

Murray, H.A. (1938). *Explorations in personality.* New York: Oxford University Press.

Namir, S., Wolcott, D.L., Fawzy, F.I., & Alumbaugh, M.J. (1987). Coping with AIDS: Psychological and health implications. *Journal of Applied Social Psychology, 17,* 309-328.

Nichols, S.E. (1985). Psychosocial reactions of persons with acquired immunodeficiency syndrome. *Annals of Internal Medicine, 103,* 765-767.

Ostrow, D., Emmons, C.A., & Altman, N.L. (1985). Sexual behavior change and persistence in homosexual men. In *Proceedings of the First International Conference on the Acquired Immunodeficiency Syndrome (AIDS).* Atlanta, GA.

Otto, J. (1991). Befindensveränderungen durch emotionsbezogene und aufgabenbezogene Stressbewältigung. Pfaffenweiler: Centaurus.

Parker, G., Brown, L., & Blignault, I. (1986). Coping behaviors as predictors of the course of clinical depression. *Archives of General Psychiatry, 43,* 561-565.

Patry, J.-L., & Perrez, M. (1982). Entstehungs-, Erklärungs- und Anwendungszusammenhang technologischer Regeln. In J.-L. Patry (Hrsg.), *Feldforschung* (S. 389-412). Bern: Huber.

Patterson, G.R. (1982). *Coercive family process. A social learning approach.* Oregon: Castalia.

Pawlik, K., & Buse, L. (1982). Rechnergestützte Verhaltensregistrierung im Feld: Beschreibung und erste psychometrische Überprüfung einer neuen Erhebungsmethode. *Zeitschrift für Differentielle und Diagnostische Psychologie, 3,* 101-118.

Perrez, M. (1984). *Streßverarbeitung bei neurotisch Depressiven. Wie sie handeln und wie sie handeln sollten. Theorie und empirische Befunde* (Forschungsbericht Nr. 50). Freiburg/Schweiz, Universität, Psychologisches Institut.

Perrez, M., Malacrida, R., Bomio, D., & Matathia, R. (1988). *Psychological stressors in medical care* (Forschungsbericht Nr. 72). Freiburg/Schweiz, Universität, Psychologisches Institut.

Perrez, M., & Patry, J.-L. (1982): Nomologisches Wissen, technologisches Wissen, Tatsachenwissen - drei Ziele sozialwissenschaftlicher Forschung. In J.-L. Patry (Hrsg.), *Feldforschung* (S. 389-412). Bern: Huber.

Perrez, M., & Reicherts, M. (1986). Appraisal, coping, and attribution processes by depressed persons: An S-R-S-R approach. In The German Journal of Psychology, 10, 315-326.

Perrez, M., & Reicherts, M. (1987a). Behavior and cognition analysis of coping with stress by depressed persons. A criterion- and process-oriented measurement approach. In W. Huber (Ed.), *Progress in Psychotherapy Research* (pp. 115-133). Louvain-La-Neuve: Presses Universitaires.

Perrez, M., & Reicherts, M. (1987b). Coping behavior in the natural setting: A method of computer-aided self-observation. In H.-P. Dauwalder, M. Perrez & V. Hobi (eds.), *Controversial issues in behavior modification* (pp. 127-137). Lisse: Swets & Zeitlinger.

Perrez, M., Reicherts, M., & Plancherel, B. (1990). Belastungsbewältigung bei HIV-Positiven. Moderatoreffekte zwischen Belastung und psychischer Gesundheit. In *Schweizerische Zeitschrift für Psychologie, 49,* 48-56.

Pervin, L.A., & Lewis, M. (Eds.). *Perspectives in interactional psychology.* New York: Plenum Press.

Platt, J.J., & Spivack, G. (1974). Means of solving real life problems: Psychiatric patients vs. controls and cross-cultural comparison of normal females. *Journal of Community Psychology, 2,* 45-48.

Popper, K.R., & Eccles, R. (1977). *The self and its brain.* New York: Springer.

Reicherts, M. (1986). *BS-J. Bewältigung belastender Situationen bei Jugendlichen. Mehrdimensionaler situationsspezifischer S-R-Fragebogen* (Forschungsbericht Nr. 62). Freiburg/Schweiz: Universität, Psychologisches Institut.

Reicherts, M. (1988). *Diagnostik der Belastungsverarbeitung. Neue Zugänge zu Stress-Bewältigungs-Prozessen.* Bern: Huber.

Reicherts, M., & Perrez, M. (1990). Einflüsse von Repression und Sensitization auf die Selbstbeobachtung der Belastungsverarbeitung. *Zeitschrift für Klinische Psychologie, Psychopathologie und Psychotherapie, 38,* 324-333.

Reicherts, M., & Perrez, M. (1991). *Fragebogen zum Umgang mit Belastungen im Verlauf (UBV). Fragebogen und Handanweisung.* Bern: Huber.

Reicherts, M., & Diethelm, K. (1988). *Assessing rule-oriented behavior: A new methodology* (Forschungsbericht Nr. 71). Freiburg/Schweiz: Universität, Psychologisches Institut.

Reicherts, M., Käslin, S., & Perrez, M. (1984). *Stressbewältigung.* Erster Arbeitsbericht der Entwicklung eines kriteriumsorientierten psychodiagnostischen Verfahrens zur theoriegeleiteten Analyse sozialängstlichen und depressiven Verhaltens (Forschungsbericht Nr. 45). Freiburg/Schweiz, Universität.

Reicherts, M., Perrez, M., & Matathia, R. (1986). *COMES. Computergestütztes Erfassungs-System. Manual.* Freiburg/Schweiz: Universität, Psychologisches Institut.

Reicherts, M., Schedle, A., & Diethelm, K. (1989). *Zum Umgang mit Problemsituationen in der frühen Mutter-Kind-Interaktion. Konzeption, Validität und Reliabilität eines S-R-Prozessfragebogens für Mütter (UBV-MK).* Freiburg/Schweiz: Universität, Psychologisches Institut.

Rippere, V. (1979). Scaling the helpfulness of antidepressive activities. *Behaviour Research and Therapy, 17,* 439-449.

Robinson, J.A., & Lewis, D.J. (1989). Coping with ICU work-related stressors: A study. *Critical Care Nurse, 10,* 80-88.

Rosenthal, R., & Rubin, D.B. (1982). A simple, general purpose display of magnitude of experimental effect. *Journal of Educational Psychology, 74,* 166-169.

Rotter, J.B. (1966). Generalized expectancies for internal versus external control of reinforcement. *Psychological Monographs: General and Applied, 80,* (Whole No. 609).

Rotter, J.B. (1972). An introduction to social learning theory. In J.B. Rotter, J.E. Chance & J.E. Phares (Eds.), *Applications of a social learning theory of personality* (pp. 1-43). New York: Holt, Rinehart & Winston.

Scherer, K.R. (1984). On the nature and function of emotion: A component process approach. In K.R. Scherer & P. Ekman (eds.), *Approaches to emotion* (pp. 293-317). Hillsdale, NJ: Erlbaum.

Scherer, K.R. (1988). Criteria for emotion-antecedent appraisal: A review. In V. Hamilton et al. (eds.), *Cognitive perspectives on emotion and motivation* (pp. 89-126). Kluwer Academic Publisher.

Scherer, K.R., Wallbott, H.G., Tolkmitt, F.J., & Bergmann, G. (1985). *Die Streßreaktion: Physiologie und Verhalten*. Göttingen: Hogrefe.

Schiefer-Hoffmann, E. (1986). *Die Bedeutung psychologischer, psychosozialer und psychosomatischer Co-Faktoren für den Verlauf der HTLV-3 Infektion. Eine prospektive psychoneuroimmunologische Untersuchung mit männlichen homosexuellen Personen*. Unveröff. Diplomarbeit. Darmstadt: Technische Hochschule.

Schlicht, W., Meyer, N., & Janssen, J.P. (1990). Ich will mein Rennen laufen. Bewältigung belastender Ereignisse im Triathlon - Eine Pilotstudie. *Sportpsychologie, 4*, Heft 1, 5-14 & Heft 2, 5-9.

Schmidt, L.R., Schwenkmezger, P., & Dlugosch, G.E. (1990). The scope of health psychology. In L.R. Schmidt, P. Schwenkmezger, P., Weinmann, J. & S. Maes (eds.), *Theoretical and applied aspects of Health Psychology* (pp. 3-28). Chur: Harwood Academic Publ.

Schönpflug, W. (1985). Goal directed behavior as a source of stress: Psychological origins and consequences of inefficiency. In M. Frese & J. Sabini (eds.), *Goal directed behavior: The concept of action in psychology* (pp. 172-188). Hillsdale, NJ: Erlbaum.

Schönpflug, W., & Battmann, W. (1988). The costs and benefits of coping. In S. Fisher & J. Reason (Eds.), Handbook of life stress (pp. 699-713. New York: Wiley.

Schroder, H.M., Driver, M.J., & Streufert, S. (1967). *Human information processing: individuals and groups functioning in complex social situations*. New York: Holt.

Schwenkmezger, P. (1991). Persönlichkeit und Wohlbefinden. In A. Abele & P. Becker (Hrsg.), Wohlbefinden: Theorie, Empirie, Diagnostik (S. 119-137). München: Juventa.

Schwenkmezger, P., & Schmitz-Friedhoff, K. (1987). Tagesablauf und Persönlichkeit. *Trierer Psychologische Berichte, 14* (5). Trier: Universität.

Seligman, M.E.P. (1975). *Helplessness. On depression, development, and death*. San Francisco: Freeman & Comp.

Silber, E., Hamburg,, D.A., Coelho, G.V., Murphy, E.B., Rosenberg, M., & Pearlin, L.I. (1961). Adaptive behavior in competent adolescents. *Archives of General Psychiatry, 5*, 354-365.

Spielberger, C.D., Gorsuch, R.L., & Lushene, R. (1970). STAI: Manual for the state-trait anxiety inventory. Palo Alto: Psychological Press.

Stegmüller, W. (1983). *Probleme und Resultate der Wissenschaftstheorie und Analytischen Philosophie.* Berlin: Springer.

Tross, S., & Hirsch, A.D. (1988). Psychological Distress and neuropsychological complications of HIV infection and AIDS. *American Psychologist, 43,* 929-934.

Tross, S., Holland, J., Hirsch, D.A., Schiffman, M., Gold, J., & Safai, B. (1986). Psychological and social impact of AIDS spectrum disorders. *Proceedings of the Second International Conference on Acquired Immunodeficiency Syndrome (AIDS)* (p. 157). Paris, France: Voyage Conseil.

Ulrich, P. (1987). *Psychische Gesundheit und Belastungsverarbeitung bei Jugendlichen mit besonderer Berücksichtigung der Cannabis-Konsumenten.* Unveröff. Dissertation, Universität Freiburg/Schweiz.

Ullrich, R., & Ullrich de Muynck, R. (Hrsg.) (1978). *Soziale Kompetenz* (Bd. 1). München: Pfeiffer.

Trautmann-Sponsel, R.D. (1988). Depression und antidepressives Verhalten. In L. Brüderl (Hrsg.), *Theorien und Methoden der Bewältigungsforschung* (S. 107-114). München: Juventa.

Vaillant, G.E. (1976). Natural history of male psychological health. The relation of choice of ego mechanisms of defense to adult adjustment. *Archives of General Psychiatry, 33,* 535-545.

Weber, H., & Laux, L. (1990). *Intentionen in der Bewältigung: Entwurf einer systematischen Taxonomie.* Memorandum Nr. 7, Lehrstuhl für Persönlichkeitspsychologie, Universität Bamberg.

Weber, H., & Laux, L. (1991). Bewältigung und Wohlbefinden. In A. Abele-Brehm & P. Becker (Hrsg.), *Wohlbefinden: Theorie-Empirie-Diagnostik* (S. 139-154). Weinheim/München: Juventa.

Weiner, B. (1982). An attributionally based theory of motivation and emotion: Focus, range, and issues. In N.T. Feather (ed.), *Expectations and actions: Expectancy-value models in psychology.* Hillsdale, NJ: Lawrence Erlbaum.

Wieberg, H.-J.W. (1983). Probleme kriteriumsorientierter Leistungsmessung: Sicherung der Kontentvalidität. In R. Horn, K. Ingenkamp, R.S. Jäger (Hrsg.), *Tests und Trends, 3. Jahrbuch der Pädagogischen Diagnostik* (S. 29-52). Weinheim: Beltz.

Wiedl, K.H., Schöttner, B., & Schöttke, H. (1990). Krankheitsbewältigung als Befolgung technologischer Regeln. Eine Analyse des
Bewältigungsverhaltens schizophrener Patienten. *Zeitschrift für
Klinische Psychologie, Psychopathologie und Psychotherapie, 38,* 334-
341.

White, R.W. (1959). Motivation reconsidered: The concept of competence. *Psychological Review, 66,* 297-333.

White, R.W. (1974). Strategies of adaptation: An attempt at systematic
description. In G.V. Coelho, D. Hamburg & J.E. Adams (eds.),
Coping and adaptation. New York: Basic Books.

Zeitlin, S. (1980). Assessing coping behavior. *American Journal of Ortho-
psychiatry, 50,* 139-144.

Some parts of this book are reworked versions of the following publications:

Chapter 2: Reicherts, M. (1988). *Diagnostik der Belastungsverarbeitung.
Neue Zugänge zu Stress-Bewältigungs-Prozessen.* Bern: Huber.
(chapter 4).

Chapter 4: Perrez, M., & Reicherts, M. (1987). Coping behavior in the
natural setting: A method of computer-aided self-observation. In
H.-P. Dauwalder, M. Perrez, & V. Hobi (eds.), *Controversial issues in behavior modification* (pp. 127-137). Lisse: Swets & Zeitlinger.

Chapter 5: Reicherts, M., & Perrez, M. (1989). Prediction of behavior
in the natural setting. In J.A. Keats, R. Taft, R.A. Heath & S.H.
Lovibond (Eds.), *Mathematical and Theoretical Systems* (pp. 111-
121). Amsterdam: Elsevier North-Holland.

Chapter 6: Perrez, M., & Reicherts, M. (1986). Appraisal, coping, and
attribution processes by depressed persons: An S-R-S-R approach.
The German Journal of Psychology, 10, 315-326.

Chapter 7: Reicherts, M., Käslin, S., Scheurer, F., Fleischhauer, J., &
Perrez, M. (1987). Belastungsverarbeitung bei endogen Depressi-
ven. *Zeitschrift für Klinische Psychologie, Psychopathologie und
Psychotherapie, 35,* 197-210.

Chapter 9: Perrez, M. (1988). Bewältigung von Alltagsbelastungen und
seelische Gesundheit. Zusammenhänge auf der Grundlage compu-
ter-unterstützter Selbstbeobachtungs- und Fragebogendaten. *Zeitschrift für Klinische Psychologie, 17,* 292-306.

Appendix

Stress and Coping Process Questionnaire (SCPQ)

by Michael Reicherts and Meinrad Perrez (1991)

The development and the structure of the Stress and Coping Process Questionnaire is described in detail in chapter 2. In the following the *final version* of the SPCQ is presented. The *2 response forms* refer to the two types of episodes: *aversive* situations and situations of *loss and failure*. Each *response* corresponds to one variable, the different numbers of responses represent different variables (e.g. rating response no. 5 operationalizes 'controllability'). The phases of the episodes listed below are to be merged into the episode 'windows' at the top of the left hand page. The type of situation (aversive vs. loss/failure) has to fit the type of response form.

The whole version contains 18 episodes, with 3 phases each (onset, continuation, outcome). A *screening version* of the SCPQ refers to 4 aversive episodes: No. 3, 9, 10 and 12).

The first episode response form presented (pp. 214-219) is for the *aversive situations:* episodes no. 1, 3, 6, 8, 9, 10, 12, 14, 16.

The second response form (pp. 220-225) is for the situations of *loss and failure:* episodes no. 2, 4, 5, 7, 8, 11, 13, 17, 18.

Episodes 1, 3, 4, 5, 8, 11, 14, 17, and 18 describe a *positive outcome* in phase 3, episodes 2, 6, 7, 9, 10, 12, 13, 15, and 16 a *negative* outcome.

Results are analysed according to the procedure described in chapter 3.

Episode No. 1

phase 1: onset
You have forgotten to do something important for your partner. You became aware of it just at the moment when your partner asks about it. Your partner gets very angry and blames you.

phase 2: continuation
After a while your partner's attitude to you has hardly changed: he/she is still angry and he still blames you for your mistake.

phase 3: outcome
At least your partner has apologized for having been so vehement. You work together to try and find a way to repair the damage.

Episode No. 2

A person who was very close to you, especially in recent times, has to move away unexpectedly. When you parted you reassured each other you would both keep in close contact. But his/her new home is quite far away. You could see each other only rarely, if at all.

In the meantime, some weeks have passed. The person hasn't got in touch with you again. Nevertheless, you feel from time to time that you miss her/him.

Finally it has become clear that your friendship isn't the same any more. Your relationship with other people can't replace what you have lost. Now and then you feel disappointed about the relationship you have lost.

Episode No. 3

You are together with some colleagues. One says that you don't pull your weight when there is difficult work. He claims that you don't think of other colleagues.

Some time later another colleague hints that the problem is not that you don't think of others, but that you lack any real interest in the work.

Finally you realise what your colleagues were really getting at, and you, for your part, were able to convince them, that you sometimes are more cautious at work than others.

Episode No. 4

You cannot find something which is very precious to you. It is associated with the memory of someone who is/was important for you. You have to face up to the possibility that you have lost it.

Meanwhile time has passed. The missing object which is so important for you did not appear again.

The object seems to definitively be lost. However, you manage to accept this by thinking of other things and memories which are just as precious to you.

Episode No. 5

You have invested a lot of time and effort in a work project. It is really important for you, that you finish this work in a few days and that it is done well. Then you realize that important material is not available. It is vital you have it in order to finish this work.

Shortly before the deadline you realize that you have not found a way to get the material you need so badly.

In the end, you concentrated more on other aspects of your task and made a successful job of it. You finally finished the project late, but you did your work well.

Episode No. 6

You are with others, friends and some people you don't know. You have just done something embarrassing. Somebody has noticed it and brought it to the attention of the others. All around, people are laughing at you. You can also hear some impertinent remarks.

Some time later people hadn't yet calmed. They are still making sarcastic remarks about your predicament and are still laughing about it.

People still hadn't calmed down when you left. They were still being cheeky and belittling regarding your mistake.

Episode No. 7

Your work place will soon be reorganized. When it happens you should finish one aspect of your work you have being doing until now. It is work which is very familiar to you and which you have mastered. In its place, you will have to take on other tasks which are as yet undefined and probably not so easy for you to do. You will miss your previous work very much.

After a trial period the new set-up becomes definite. Your work place is to be reorganized. The new tasks you have taken over are rather difficult for you and don't satisfy you. You are really missing your previous work.

You didn't get on very well with your new work. You miss your previous work very much. Other aspects of your work don't compensate for this.

Episode No. 8

Walking down a crowded street, you strike a parked car with your bag. The driver, who was just about to get in, inspects his car. He becomes very angry and blames you for having scratched the car. He becomes abusive towards you and wants you to pay for the damage.

The driver continues to be very angry. Again he loudly demands that you should pay for the damage.

The driver remained fairly angry. But finally he seemed to accept that the scratches on his car were hardly likely to have been made by your bag.

Episode No. 9

Previous relations with your boss have been quite complicated. Now your boss gives you a task which you are supposed to work for the next two days. This job is very inconvenient for you because you have a lot of routine work to do at the moment.

Your boss tells you that your routine work also has to be done. As you begin to work on the new task, it becomes evident how difficult and timeconsuming it really is. It seems that you will only finish it if you ignore your other work, and even then you may have to do overtime on it.

You didn't carry out the job in the assigned time. Also a lot of routine work remained unfinished.

Episode No. 10

You have just got to know someone you find pretty sympathetic. You have met several times and got on well together. Now you are talking about something which is important to you. The other person does not agree at all and says that your ideas and arguments seem "rather strange" to her.

Later the person says that she really goes to great lengths to understand you, but she does not manage to agree with you. Obviously you could talk about this for a long time, she says, but maybe both of you see the world differently.

The disagreements between you remained until the end of your meeting. It was never clear to you what the disagreement was actually about.

Episode No. 11

Your firm recently advertised a very interesting job. You have the impression that you would be a possible candidate with your professional qualifications. For different reasons you are hesitating to apply, although a fast decision is needed. Now you hear that one of your colleagues has applied for this job. He is qualified for the job, but you don't like him.

Some days later you hear that your colleague will probably will get the job. It seems that he has only to accept the offer.

Your colleague has got the job. Meanwhile, you have concentrated successfully on other tasks. You have already heard that soon new professional opportunities will be offered which may be of interest to you.

Episode No. 12

You and your partner have been having a difficult time together over the past few weeks. On several occasions you could have criticised your partner without saying something. Now she/he is saying that she/he find you 'very disagreeable' at present.

Later your partner is repeating his/her vague reproach. You have only a vague idea as to the background of his/her remark. Your partner seems to be avoiding giving you an explanation.

It remains unclear what your partner means by his/her vague reproaches. You can only guess at the reasons. The mutual reproaches are continuing.

Episode No. 13

You are unable to find an important document which details your professional qualification. You need it urgently.

After a few days, the missing document still hasn't appeared. It is highly important that you should always have this document at your disposal.

You could not find the certificate in time. You had to show your credentials in another, less satisfactory way.

Episode No. 14

Your work colleagues are discussing a professional question in your presence. Although the topic concerns your job and you are familiar with the matter, they don't attach any importance to your opinion. You have just given your opinion, but your colleagues don't take really notice what you have said.

The discussion is continuing. Your colleagues still disregard your opinion.

Finally you have succeeded to make your opinion known. Some of your colleagues have fully accepted your arguments.

Episode No. 15

You don't have a good relationship with your landlord. Now he tells you that he is considering cancelling your lease. Probably he will need your home for his own use. You are used to the flat and you like the place and its location.

Not far from the prescribed cancellation time your landlord tells you that he is probably going to cancel the lease and to use the flat himself.

You have now to move out and you could not find a similar flat in the vicinity.

Episode No. 16

You have a problem at work. A new colleague that you don't yet know well is passing and is having a look at your work. Without being unfriendly he implies that your work could be done in another, more efficient way.

The new colleague is explaining in a challenging way how the work can be done differently. It is not clear to you what he means. He then adds that there may be different ways to solve the problem, but he stresses his 'own experiences in the area'.

It remains unclear to you if your colleague's suggestion is valuable or not. His provocative behaviour also seems ambiguous to you.

Episode No. 17

You are planning a journey. You intend to visit good friends who live far away. You have not met for a long time, and you have invested a lot of time and energy to ensure the trip came about. Now you receive the message that your visit has possibly to be cancelled because of an illness in your friends' family.

The day before your departure you are receive the message from your friends that it would probably better to postpone your visit, because of the illness in their family. If you postpone the journey, it would be for an indefinite time.

Finally you could not visit your friends. You have changed your program, and you have fixed with your friends a new date for the visit.

Episode No. 18

A work colleague has recently left your firm. His departure surprised you. You worked well with him and you have received a lot of professional support from him. When he was leaving you both agreed to remain in contact and to continue the professional exchange.

Meanwhile time passed. After one only spontaneous contact by phone you have never heard anything from him. Nevertheless you continue to feel that you are missing his cooperation and support.

The professional exchange is indeed not the same as in former times, but from time to time you continue to have contact with your colleague and you meet occasionally. You have also begun to cooperate with other colleagues at the firm and you receive a lot of professional support from them.

Try and clearly imagine the following situation:

```

```

In this situation **I feel:**   very   fairly rather rather fairly very

1)   nervous/anxious   0   1   2   3   4   5   calm/composed

2)   depressed/sad   0   1   2   3   4   5   cheerful/serene

3)   angry/furious   0   1   2   3   4   5   gentle/peaceful

My judgements *about this situation are as follows:*

		very small	small	rather small	rather large	large	very large
4)	the chances of this situation taking a turn for the better without effort on my part are	0	1	2	3	4	5
5)	the chances that I can influence this situation for the better are	0	1	2	3	4	5
6)	the overall amount of stress for me in this situation is	0	1	2	3	4	5

7)   I have experienced a similar situation

	0	1	2	3	4	5
	never before	once	rarely	some-times	often	very often

In this situation **my intentions** *are as follows:*

		not important at all	not very important	rather important	very important
8)	to actively confront the other(s) and to clear up what is at stake	0	1	2	3
9)	to maintain a friendly atmosphere and to prevent an argument with the other(s)	0	1	2	3
12)	to remain calm and composed	0	1	2	3
13)	to keep my self-esteem	0	1	2	3

Please mark <u>for every question</u> the number you feel is most appropriate for you!

In this situation **my actions** *are as follows:*	not at all	hardly	perhaps	probably	certainly
14) I fade out, stop paying attention or look for distractions	0	1	2	3	4
15) I make clear to myself what is at stake and what I should do	0	1	2	3	4
16) I make clear to myself that this situation is <u>not</u> as straining/important as other problems	0	1	2	3	4
17) I get my emotions under control (be positive, relax, take a drink, a cigarette etc.)	0	1	2	3	4
18) I blame or reproach the other(s) [or circumstances] by myself	0	1	2	3	4
19) I blame or reproach myself	0	1	2	3	4
	not at all	hardly	perhaps	probably	certainly
23) I behave passively or wait for something to happen	0	1	2	3	4
24) I try to withdraw from the situation (e.g. by avoiding certain things/people or turning away)	0	1	2	3	4
25) I try to actively influence the situation, by doing	0	1	2	3	4

Imagine the situation carries on in the following way:

In this situation **I feel:**		very	fairly	rather	rather	fairly	very	
1)	nervous/anxious	0	1	2	3	4	5	calm/composed
2)	depressed/sad	0	1	2	3	4	5	cheerful/serene
3)	angry/furious	0	1	2	3	4	5	gentle/peaceful

My judgments *about this situation as follows:*	very small	small	rather small	rather large	large	very large
4) the chances of this situation taking a turn for the better without effort on my part is	0	1	2	3	4	5
5) the chances that I can influence this situation for the better are	0	1	2	3	4	5
6) the overall amount of stress for me in this situation is	0	1	2	3	4	5

In this situation **my intentions** *are as follows:*	not important at all	not very important	rather important	very important
8) to actively confront the other(s) and to clear up what is at stake	0	1	2	3
9) to maintain a friendly atmosphere and to prevent an argument with the other(s)	0	1	2	3
12) to remain calm and composed	0	1	2	3
13) to keep my self-esteem	0	1	2	3

Please mark for every question the number most appropriate for you!

In this situation **my actions** *are as follows:*	not at all	hardly	perhaps	probably	certainly
14) I fade out, stop paying attention or look for distractions	0	1	2	3	4
15) I make clear to myself what is at stake and what I should do	0	1	2	3	4
16) I make clear to myself that this situation is not as straining/important as other problems	0	1	2	3	4
17) I get my emotions under control (be positive, relax, take a drink, a cigarette etc.)	0	1	2	3	4
18) I blame or reproach the other(s) [or circumstances] by myself	0	1	2	3	4
19) I blame or reproach myself	0	1	2	3	4
	not at all	hardly	perhaps	probably	certainly
23) I behave passively or wait for something to happen	0	1	2	3	4
24) I try to withdraw from the situation (e.g. by avoiding certain things/people or turning away)	0	1	2	3	4
25) I try to actively influence the situation, by doing	0	1	2	3	4

....

Imagine the situation finally turns out as follows:

```



```

In this situation **I feel**:

		very	fairly	rather	rather	fairly	very	
1)	nervous/anxious	0	1	2	3	4	5	calm/composed
2)	depressed/sad	0	1	2	3	4	5	cheerful/serene
3)	angry/furious	0	1	2	3	4	5	gentle/peaceful

	very small	small	rather small	rather large	large	very large
6) the overall amount of stress for me in this situation is	0	1	2	3	4	5

I would **attribute** *the outcome of this situation:*

	not at all	in part	rather	entirely
29) to my own behavior	0	1	2	3
30) to the behavior of the other(s)	0	1	2	3
31) to circumstances	0	1	2	3

Please mark <u>for every question</u> the number you feel is most appropriate for you!

I would then <u>do</u> the following:	not at all	hardly	perhaps	probably	certainly
14) I distance myself from what happened, stop paying attention or look for distractions	0	1	2	3	4
15) I make clear to myself what was at stake and what I better could have done better	0	1	2	3	4
16) I make clear to myself that this situation was <u>not</u> as straining/important as other problems	0	1	2	3	4
17) I get my emotions under control (be positive, relax, take a drink, a cigarette etc.)	0	1	2	3	4
20) I say to myself, after all that, I did quite well	0	1	2	3	4
21) I talk to an intimate friend or another person about it	0	1	2	3	4
22) I intend to make it different next time, by doing	0	1	2	3	4

....

Try and clearly imagine the following situation:

```


```

In this situation **I feel**·   very   fairly rather rather fairly very

1)	nervous/anxious	0	1	2	3	4	5	calm/composed
2)	depressed/sad	0	1	2	3	4	5	cheerful/serene
3)	angry/furious	0	1	2	3	4	5	gentle/peaceful

My judgments *about this situation are as follows:*

	very small	small	rather small	rather large	large	very large
4) the chances of this situation taking a turn for the better without effort on my part are	0	1	2	3	4	5
5) the chances that I can influence this situation for the better are	0	1	2	3	4	5
6) the overall amount of stress for me in this situation is	0	1	2	3	4	5
7) I have experienced a similar situation	0 never before	1 once	2 rarely	3 some- times	4 often	5 very often

In this situation **my intentions** *are as follows:*

	not impor- tant at all	not very important	rather important	very important
10) to maintain the relationship [or objective] which is at stake	0	1	2	3
11) to find alternative relationships [or objectives]	0	1	2	3
12) to remain calm and composed	0	1	2	3
13) to keep my self-esteem	0	1	2	3

Please mark for every question the number you feel most appropriate for you!

*In this situation **my actions** are as follows:*	not at all	hardly	perhaps	probably	certainly
14) I fade out, stop paying attention or look for distractions	0	1	2	3	4
15) I make clear to myself what is at stake and what I should do	0	1	2	3	4
16) I make clear to myself that this situation is not as straining/important as other problems	0	1	2	3	4
17) I get my emotions under control (be positive, relax, take a drink, a cigarette etc.)	0	1	2	3	4
18) I blame or reproach the other(s) [or circumstances] by myself	0	1	2	3	4
19) I blame or reproach myself	0	1	2	3	4

	not at all	hardly	perhaps	probably	certainly
26) I behave passively or wait for something to happen	0	1	2	3	4
27) I try to actively prevent a loss or a failure, by doing	0	1	2	3	4
28) I try to actively re-orientate my position (e.g. by focusing on other relationships, things, projects), by doing	0	1	2	3	4

Imagine the situation carries on in the following way:

In this situation **I feel:**   very   fairly rather rather fairly very

1)	nervous/anxious	0	1	2	3	4	5	calm/composed
2)	depressed/sad	0	1	2	3	4	5	cheerful/serene
3)	angry/furious	0	1	2	3	4	5	gentle/peaceful

My judgement *about this situation are as follows:*

		very small	small	rather small	rather large	large	very large
4)	the chances of this situation taking a turn for the better without effort on my part are	0	1	2	3	4	5
5)	the chances that I can influence this situation for the better are	0	1	2	3	4	5
6)	the overall amount of stress for me in this situation is	0	1	2	3	4	5

In this situation **my intentions** *are as follows:*

		not important at all	not very important	rather important	very important
10)	to keep up the relationship [or objective] which is at stake	0	1	2	3
11)	to find alternative relationships [or objectives]	0	1	2	3
12)	to remain calm and composed	0	1	2	3
13)	to keep my self-esteem	0	1	2	3

Please mark for every question the number most appropriate for you!

In this situation **my actions** *are as follows:*	not at all	hardly	perhaps	probably	certainly
14) I fade out, stop paying attention or look for distractions	0	1	2	3	4
15) I make clear to myself what is at stake and what I should do	0	1	2	3	4
16) I make clear to myself that this situation is not as straining/important as other problems	0	1	2	3	4
17) I get my emotions under control (be positive, relax, take a drink, a cigarette etc.)	0	1	2	3	4
18) I blame or reproach the other(s) [or circumstances] by myself	0	1	2	3	4
19) I blame or reproach myself	0	1	2	3	4

	not at all	hardly	perhaps	probably	certainly
26) I behave passively or wait for something to happen	0	1	2	3	4
27) I try to actively prevent a loss or a failure, by doing	0	1	2	3	4
28) I try to actively re-orientate my position (e.g. by focusing on other relationships, things, projects), by doing	0	1	2	3	4

Imagine the situation <u>finally turns out as follows:</u>

```
┌────────────────────────────────────────────────────────────────────┐
│                                                                    │
│                                                                    │
│                                                                    │
│                                                                    │
│                                                                    │
└────────────────────────────────────────────────────────────────────┘
```

Then I feel: very   fairly rather rather fairly very

		very	fairly	rather	rather	fairly	very	
1)	nervous/anxious	0	1	2	3	4	5	calm/composed
2)	depressed/sad	0	1	2	3	4	5	cheerful/serene
3)	angry/furious	0	1	2	3	4	5	gentle/peaceful

	very small	small	rather small	rather large	large	very large
6) the overall amount of stress for me in this situation is	0	1	2	3	4	5

I would <u>attribute</u> the outcome of this situation:

	not at all	in part	rather	entirely
29) to my own behavior	0	1	2	3
30) to the behavior of the other(s)	0	1	2	3
31) to circumstances	0	1	2	3

Please mark <u>for every question</u> the number most appropriate for You!

I would then <u>do</u> the following:	not at all	hardly	perhaps	probably	certainly
14) I distance myself from what happened, stop paying attention or look for distractions	0	1	2	3	4
15) I make clear to myself what was at stake and what I would have done better	0	1	2	3	4
16) I make clear to myself that this situation was <u>not</u> as straining/important as other problems	0	1	2	3	4
17) I get my emotions under control (be positive, relax, take a drink, a cigarette etc.)	0	1	2	3	4
20) I say to myself, after all that, I did quite well	0	1	2	3	4
21) I talk to an intimate friend or another person about it	0	1	2	3	4
22) I intend to make it different next time, by doing	0	1	2	3	4

*COM*puter-assisted *RE*cording *S*ystem (COMRES)

by Meinrad Perrez, Michael Reicherts and Robert Matathia (1987)

Program structures (BASIC)

(Appendix) Figure 1. Question/answer interaction during text input (basic structure)

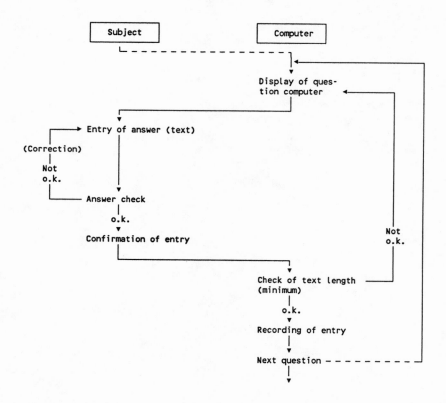

(Appendix) Figure 2. Question/answer interaction for scaled input (basic structure)

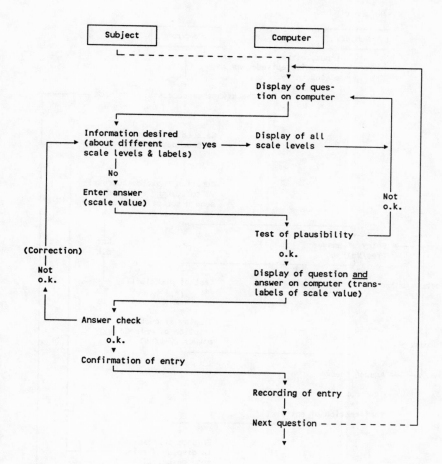

(Appendix) Figure 3. Question/answer interaction in episode linking (basic structure)

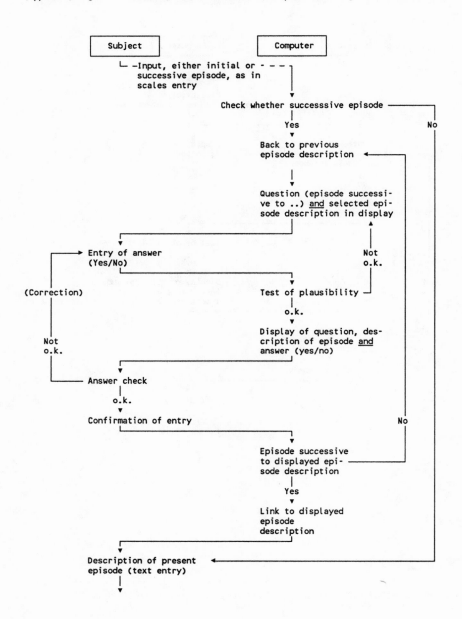

Subject index